CARD GAMES
FOR ONE

David Parlett

TEACH YOURSELF BOOKS

Hodder and Stoughton

To Patricia

First published 1986
Second impression 1988

British Library Cataloguing in Publication Data

Parlett, David
    Card games for one. – (Teach yourself books)
    1. Solitaire (Game)
    I. Title
    795.4'3   GV1261

ISBN 0 340 39967 8

Printed and bound in Great Britain
for Hodder and Stoughton Educational,
a division of Hodder and Stoughton Ltd,
Mill Road, Dunton Green, Sevenoaks, Kent,
by Richard Clay Ltd, Bungay, Suffolk
Photoset by Rowland Phototypesetting Ltd,
Bury St Edmunds, Suffolk.

Contents

Games for Three or More Packs

Introduction

Card games for one player are called Patience or Solitaire, depending on where you live and what language you speak. There are
hundreds of different species of Patience, though it seems to be a
fact of life that most players know only one or two of them. In this
book I will introduce you to about 150 different ways of playing the
pack of cards, and I have gone out of my way to make the selection
as *varied* as possible. Not that I'm suggesting you should regularly
play them all – life is too short for that – but rather because I think
the more you experiment with different games, the likelier you are
to find one or two that seem to be specially designed to appeal to
your own particular tastes and will therefore bring you the greatest
possible enjoyment. I have my own favourites, of course, and
probably have not disguised my dislikes very well; but I am sure you
will not let that stop you making up your own mind about individual
games.

The book is divided into three parts. The first contains games
played with a single 52-card pack, the second those requiring a
doubled pack of 104 cards, and the third containing a handful of
games using three or more packs of either 52 or 32 cards each. Such
a division is technically artificial as there are many instances in
which what is virtually the same game is played with either one or
two packs and has a different title in each case. But it is convenient
to the practical player, who may have a preference for one- or
two-pack games, or who may not wish to go to the expense of
having three packs and therefore has to keep separating the cards
according to the number required.

Within each section I have grouped together games which go
together by similarity of theme or structure, so that if you find one
you like (or dislike), you will find similar ones to try (or avoid) on
the neighbouring pages. Also, very broadly speaking, the order of
games in the two main sections is from comparatively trivial to
relatively deep. This means that if you are looking for games
requiring the highest degree of skill and intelligence, you ought to

start at the end of each section and work backwards – or, if you prefer to go forwards, start approximately in the middle. In any case, to be on the safe side, I have prefaced each game or group of games with some indication of the degree of skill required.

I should say something about what I have omitted from this collection. I have not included things which come under the category of puzzles or problems with playing-cards. For example, many old books describe under the title 'Caesar' the task of arranging numeral cards from 1 to 9 in a 3 × 3 square such that every row, column and three-card diagonal adds up to fifteen. This is clearly not a game but a puzzle – once you have solved it (or looked the answer up) it loses interest. I have also omitted a number of games which require no skill at all, or are too complicated to describe for the small amount of intelligence they do manage to offer. And, of course, for the sake of variety I have avoided putting together too many games of a very similar type and differing from one another only in minor details.

Patience is best played with proper Patience cards, which are smaller than those used for competitive card games. Since the object of most games is to get the cards into suit and numerical order, it is important to shuffle them very thoroughly before starting a new game. (A game in which the cards come out in order is not only boring but often self-defeating, for the order in which they come out is usually the reverse of that in which they are actually needed!) One way of shuffling Patience cards is to spread them face down haphazardly over the table and slide them around one another in a circular motion with the tips of your fingers. Another is to deal them face up, very rapidly, into an odd number of piles, such as eleven or thirteen, more or less in rotation but with occasional changes of direction just to fool them. Doing this face up enables you to make such changes just in case you seem to be getting too many like cards together.

In case you have never played Patience before, it might be a good idea to introduce some of the basic principles underlying most of the games you are likely to come across. You will find, both below and throughout the book, that certain words crop up so frequently in describing the games that they almost have the status of technical terms. There's no need to learn them by heart. Where they occur in the main text I have often made their meaning plain in a bracketed note. They are also listed alphabetically and explained in more detail on page 144, so that you can refer to them if necessary when you are following the individual game descriptions.

It helps to regard any Patience game as consisting of an objective and a procedure, the latter being the set of rules by which the objective is to be attained. Between the two there usually comes a third component, which is the way the cards are dealt or laid out before play begins. I will say something about each of these in turn.

Objective In the average game you start with a well shuffled pack of cards and have as your object the task of putting them in order in accordance with its particular rules of play.

'In order' usually means 'in numerical order' and may also mean 'in separate suits'. A single pack normally contains 52 cards divided into four suits (spades ♠, clubs ♣, hearts ♡, diamonds ♢), each containing thirteen ranks. Numerical order means the order of ranks in each suit, which is normally as follows:

$$A\ 2\ 3\ 4\ 5\ 6\ 7\ 8\ 9\ 10\ J\ Q\ K$$

Ace is equivalent to '1', and Jack, Queen, King respectively to 11, 12 and 13. In a typical game, then, you are asked to 'found the Aces as base cards and build them up in suit and sequence to the Kings'. The result of a successful game will then be four piles, each of a given suit, with Ace at the bottom and King at the top.

Although this objective is typical, you will come across several variations on it. For example:

(a) Found the Kings as bases and build downwards in suit to the Aces. (An obvious variation, which really makes not the slightest difference to how the game goes.)

(b) In a two-pack game, found an Ace and a King of each suit, and build the Aces up to the Kings and the Kings down to the Aces. (This results in eight piles, four of 'ascending' and four of 'descending' thirteen-card sequences.)

(c) Build Aces up to Kings – or Kings down to Aces – *regardless* of suit – in other words, an Ace is followed by any Two, any Three, and so on. (This makes the task easier, of course, since the top card of a main sequence can be followed by any one of four cards instead of only one. But it may not make the

whole game easier, because some other part of it may have correspondingly more difficult rules of play.)

(d)   Found, as a base, the first card dealt, no matter what rank it is, and build upwards into a thirteen-card suit sequence. So, if the first card dealt happens to be a Ten, the sequence will go up to the Nine as follows:

10 J Q K A 2 3 4 5 6 7 8 9

When this method is specified, Aces and Kings are regarded as being consecutive.

Layout or 'tableau'   Most games start with some of the cards dealt to the table in a pattern. It may be a simple pattern like a row of columns, or a complex one intended to represent some real object as in **Fan** or **Windmill**. The undealt cards are held face down in one hand and referred to as 'the stock'. A few games start without any initial pattern, while, at the other extreme, some start with all cards dealt out so that there is no stock. On the whole, the more cards dealt to the opening layout, the more skill-demanding and less chancy the game is likely to be.

The purpose of a tableau, apart from sometimes looking pretty, may be either or both of the following. One is to make a greater variety of cards 'available' for building on the main sequences than there are if you merely turn them one by one from the top of the stock. The other, not found in all games, is to enable you to 'pack' cards on one another in reverse of building order, so that you can take them off one by one in the order required for building the main sequences.

Procedure   The rules of play then specify how cards may be moved about and packed on one another in the tableau – for example, in suit, in alternating colour, regardless of suit, and so on.

In a game where not all the cards are dealt to a layout, the rules will also specify how cards from the stock are to be entered into the game. One very common procedure is that you turn cards from the stock one by one and build them on the main sequences if you can, or pack them on the tableau if they fit, or else discard them face up to a 'wastepile' or rubbish heap. If there is a wastepile its top card is always 'available' for building or packing, so it is sometimes possible to get rid of the waste by playing all the cards off one by one as opportunities arise to get them into the game.

In many games with a wastepile, when you have played the last card of the stock, you may take up the wastepile, turn it upside down and go through it again as a new stock. This is called a 'redeal'. Games vary in the number of times a wastepile can be turned and redealt – sometimes not at all, often once, rarely more than twice.

The reason why there are so many different Patience games is that each of the three elements outlined above can be varied in several ways. For example, you may be asked to build the main sequences upwards or downwards, or both, or in some peculiar kind of numerical order, and either in suit or regardless of suit, and so on. The tableau may contain any number of rows or columns of cards, and you may or may not be allowed to 'pack' on it. If so, you may be required to pack in suit, regardless of suit, or in alternating colour, and you may or may not be allowed to move more than one card at a time. Undealt cards – the 'stock' – may be dealt to a wastepile or directly onto the tableau. If there is a wastepile, you may or may not be allowed to redeal it. You may or may not be offered a 'grace' – that is, a special move which can only be made if the game jams up and you can get no further without it.

One effect of all the variety possible in games of Patience is that you will often find no two people playing the same game in the same way, or even two authoritative books describing it in the same way. Once they get used to the ways of Patience, players find it easy to modify the rules slightly so as to make it easier or harder to bring out, or to give them more or less to think about, or to make the game faster or slower, so as to accord with their own particular tastes. A further complication arises because authors may or may not give new names to games they have produced by making such revisions and 'improvements', or they may not like (or understand) the traditional name and so change it for one of their own.

This may sound like a recipe for anarchy and confusion, but in practice it is not as bad as all that. You may find a number of almost indistinguishable games that have been derived from one another by this process of individual variation. But you will soon become aware that, as a group, they have some quite distinctive feature that sets them apart from another group of closely related games. And you may well find, as I have done, that some groups as a whole appeal more to your taste than others.

This brings us inevitably to the question of quality. Why have some games lasted longer than others, and why do some appeal to us while others leave us cold? What, in fact, makes a 'good' game of Patience?

One answer to this depends on the range of mental faculties it brings into play. I happen to like games in which all the cards are dealt face up at the start, enabling you to plan moves in advance, and so designed that they always 'come out' if you play perfectly but will always go irretrievably wrong if you make a mistake. I also prefer games with simple rather than complex rules, and one-pack rather than two-pack games because the best of them combine the qualities of elegance and miniaturism. But there are other things to look for which may appeal to you more. You may prefer games requiring memory, or those which require you to make judgments about the likelihood of certain cards turning up from the stock, or those with the uncertain element of reshuffling in mid-play. You may take more delight in the elaborate and often ingenious pictorial patterns which the Victorians were particularly prone to devising. (I like them myself, and have revived several in this book which have hardly been seen since their invention.) Not all Patience games 'come out' to provide you with a happy ending to all your labours. Some, such as **Demon** and **Miss Milligan**, remain popular in spite of – or possibly because of – their notorious reluctance to come out no matter how carefully you play.

The likelihood of a game's coming out successfully depends on one or both of two main factors. The main one, inherent in the game and so beyond your control – except by changing the rules – is the chance factor, or 'luck of the draw'. In any game you start off with a shuffled pack, follow a set of rules, and by means of them hope to finish up with an ordered pack. If the rules are friendly, or cooperative, or whatever you want to call them, they will (with proper play) enable the cards to become ordered no matter how they happen to turn up in the deal. If, however, they are tight and stingy, there are certain results of shuffling that will never come out, no matter how well or carefully you play. Throughout the book, wherever I have said that the chances are in favour or against a particular game's coming out successfully, I am assuming perfect play and giving some indication of the game's inherent friendliness.

The other factor is that of skill. In some games you are given no choices to make but simply have to play whatever is playable in accordance with very strict rules. If you have no choice, you cannot exercise skill, and such games are therefore skill-denying in the extreme – though they may demand a high degree of concentration, and very often exercise one's quality of patience, which is no bad thing in itself! Skill-demanding games, at the other extreme, are those which at almost every move give you a variety of choices to make, leaving it up to you to make the right one. Understand, though, that even a skill-demanding game will not necessarily always come out with best play. The odds may well be against it through the unfriendliness of the rules, or 'luck of the draw' factor. Throughout the book, I have given some indication of the extent to which skill comes into play for each game, in addition to its inherent likelihood of coming out.

I ought to finish this Introduction by acknowledging my sources and predecessors. Patience games seem to have first appeared in one of the Baltic states – perhaps Sweden or Germany – at the end of the eighteenth century. They reached France some time after the fall of Napoleon, thus making nonsense of all those games named after him in the mistaken belief that he would have played any of them. The earliest English collection was compiled by Lady Adelaide Cadogan and published in the early 1870s. (The BM Library knows only the second edition, dated 1875.) This was so successful that she published a second collection shortly after, in 1887. Both were based on German sources – the first through a French translation – and supplemented by a number of games of apparently English invention. Cadogan's work was continued, more cheaply but more authoritatively, by Mary Whitmore Jones, who produced at least seven collections between about 1890 and 1910. Most of the well-known and indeed classic Patience games appeared in the combined *oeuvre* of these two matriarchs.

Most Patience books produced thereafter have been second- or third-hand derivatives of games going back to Cadogan or Whitmore Jones, usually uncredited and often renamed to make them sound more origial. The first major twentieth-century contribution to the realm of Patience was made by Albert Morehead and Geoffrey Mott-Smith, whose collection was first published in the 1940s. They actually went so far as to play all the games they described, going back to source to correct them where rules had become garbled by copyists. They also improved many games by introducing elements of skill into what had previously been purely mechanical exercises, and devised a number of original Patience games of remarkable elegance and ingeniousness.

I have taken care to acknowledge the composers of individual games where they are known. Apart from those of Morehead and Mott-Smith (and a few of my own) I have also included some modern games, by Charles Jewell and Col. Latham, first published by George Hervey in the original edition of *Card Games for One*, to which this book is an enlarged and updated successor.

PART ONE
One-Pack Games

One-Pack Games

Perpetual Motion (Narcotic)

The simplest one-player card games appear to be pointless, but beware – they can become strangely addictive. That may explain the alternative title of this one, which I can only describe as a nervous activity suitable for passing the time in a dentist's waiting-room.

Keep dealing four cards in a row face up on top of the previous four. Pause after each deal. If two are of the same rank (e.g. Fives, Queens, etc.), put the right-hand one on top of the left. Repeat until no two top cards match, then deal the next four.

When you run out of cards, pick up the right-hand pile and put it on the one next to it, then place both on top of the next, and finally all on the left-hand pile. Turn them all upside-down, and start again.

Keep playing and redealing in this way. Whenever the four cards you deal in one turn are of the same rank, discard them from the game.

You win if you eventually eliminate all 52 cards. But this is unlikely to happen before they come and carry you away.

Aces Up

Also known as **Firing Squad**, and with greater honesty as **Drivel**, this game may be left to speak for itself.

As in **Perpetual Motion**, keep dealing four cards face up in a row on top of the previous four and pausing after each deal. If two or more of the top cards are of the same suit, leave the highest one in place (Ace counts higher than King) and throw the other(s) out. Keep discarding until the top cards are all of different suits, then deal the next four.

If you succeed in making a space by discarding the last card of a pile, fill it immediately with one of the other three top cards – preferably an Ace.

The game is won if you finish with four Aces in a row, having eliminated all forty-eight lower cards. As there is no redeal, however, you are unlikely to reach this happy position.

Valentine

I introduce you to *Valentine* not because it is very intelligent, but because it is very old – in case you would like to know how your ancestors managed to fritter their time away before TV quiz games were invented!

Note that Ace is low and King is high, and they are not consecutive.

Deal four cards face up in a row. If any two or more are in suit and sequence, pile them up in sequence with the lowest on top.

Turn the next card from stock. If it matches the suit of a top card and is next lower in sequence, add it to the pile. Keep turning until you get a card that does not fit.

Put this to one side as the first card of a new row of four. But before dealing the next three, gather up the previous cards or piles, turn them upside-down and add them to the bottom of the stock. Then complete the row of four and play again as described above.

You may eventually finish up with all the cards arranged in four complete suit-sequences. Pigs might also fly.

Cover-Up

A daft old game, to which I have added an even dafter refinement.

Deal four cards face up in a row. If two or more are of the same suit, cover them immediately with cards turned from stock. Keep doing this until you either run out of stock (win) or get four top cards of different suits (lose).

That is as far as the old books go, but here is a way of prolonging the torture.

If you reach a point at which all four top cards are different, leave those piles alone and continue play with a new row of four below the first. If this also sticks before you run out of cards, start a third row below the second, and so on.

Having run out of cards again, make a new stock by gathering up the piles from right to left in each row, starting at the lowest and working upwards, and turn them face down.

Keep replaying until the game either comes out in one row (win) or goes on for ever (lose).

This makes a good competitive race game, like **Pounce** or **Racing**

Demon, with each person playing their own pack until somebody wins.

Accordion

This must be a more apt title than **Methuselah**, **Tower of Babel** and the less complimentary things the game has been called in its time. If you are left-handed, keep swapping 'left' and 'right' in the following description. (If you are ambidextrous, play something else.)

Deal cards face up in a row from left to right, pausing after each to examine the situation. If the card just dealt matches the suit of the one before, or of the card next but *two* on the left, place it on top of the match.

If now the right-hand card (or the top card of the right-hand pile) matches the suit of the top card on the next or next-but-two left, put it on top and squeeze the row up to the left.

When you can match and squeeze no further, continue dealing from and to the right, and playing as described above.

If you finish with a single pile you have won. If you finish with two piles you have come second. And so on.

Accordion ♢5 goes on ♢A because it is next but two away, but ♡9 did not go on ♡J because that was only next but one. If the next card dealt is a diamond it will go on the Five; if a spade, on the Queen.

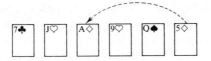

Royal Marriage

Put ♡K at the bottom of the pack and play ♡Q as the first card of a row. Continue dealing cards face up in a row to the right of the Queen. Pause after each and consider the situation. If any single card is sandwiched between two of the same suit, throw it out and squeeze the row up. Do the same of any pair of adjacent cards similarly flanked by two of a suit (but not of three or more).

If you finish with the King and Queen of hearts next to each other, you (or they) have won.

Rondo

No skill is demanded in the play of **Rondo** – otherwise known as **Eight-Day Clock** or **Perpetual Motion** – but if you have not met it before I think you will be surprised at its amusement value.

Deal thirteen cards face up in a circle, then thirteen more top of them, and so on until you have thirteen piles of four cards each. Identify one of these as the 'Ace' pile, and imagine the other twelve to be labelled from Two to King in clockwise order from it. (So, for example, the King pile will lie to the left of the Ace pile.)

If the top card of the Ace pile is not an Ace, take it and put it at the bottom of the Two pile. Then shift the top card of the Two pile to the bottom of the Three pile, the top of the Three to the bottom of the Four, and so on round the circle, with the bottom of the King pile going to the top of the Ace.

Whenever the top card of a pile matches its position in the circle (e.g. an Ace on top of the Ace pile, Two on the Two pile, etc.), leave it in place and ignore that pile from the circle, Next time round, you will slip the top card of the previous pile to the bottom of the next one which does *not* match its position.

(As you go round, you may find it helpful to announce the name of each pile as you come to it – 'Ace, Two, Three . . .', etc. – remembering to skip the pile if the card you name is at the top of it.)

Eventually, you should reach a point at which, when you lift the next card, you cannot put it anywhere because all thirteen top cards now match their positions.

When this happens, slip it half way under the next pile round. Before continuing, discard the top cards of all thirteen piles. Then carry on as before by moving the top card of the pile you just stopped at – the one with the previous stop-card sticking out.

You will quite often succeed in forming and discarding two complete thirteen-card card sequences, but you have only won if you manage to get the third out. (If the third comes out, the fourth is bound to arrange itself in order eventually, so you can take it as read.)

Don't ask me why this does – or, more usually, doesn't – happen. I only wish I knew.

Sundial

Sundial has similarities to **Rondo**, as might be suggested by such of its many alternative titles as **Clock** and **Watch** (though I think **Travellers** is equally apt).

Deal twelve cards face up in a circle, then twelve more on top of them, and keep going round until you have four left over. Put these face down to one side as a reserve.

Starting at the one o'clock position, mentally label these twelve piles Ace, Two, Three, etc. up to Jack (eleven) and Queen (twelve).

Turn the top card of the reserve and slip it underneath the pile corresponding to its rank – for example, under the Ace pile if it is an Ace, etc. Then take the top card of the pile you played to and slip it under the pile corresponding to *its* rank. Do the same again, and keep shuttling in this way until the card you are about to move is a King.

As there is no King pile, you throw the King out, take the next card of the reserve, and continue shuttling until you reach another King.

By the time you reach the fourth King you will, if successful, have got all forty-eight other cards arranged in thirteen piles in proper numerical sequence around the dial.

If not, you may, by special dispensation (for I am feeling generous today) exchange the fourth King for any card which has not yet travelled to its proper position, and continue from there.

Monte Carlo

Monte Carlo, also known as **Weddings** and **Double or Quits**, is a game of little skill but some inexplicable interest, and no collection is complete without it.

The object is to eliminate all 52 cards in pairs of the same rank.

Deal 25 cards face up in five rows of five, from left to right and top to bottom. Eliminate any two of the same rank which may be lying next to each other either side by side or diagonally.

Next, close up the gaps as follows. Fill any space with the card lying nearest to it on the right. If there is a space at the right end of a row, fill it with the first card to the left of the next row. Keep doing this until all the cards have been squeezed leftwards and upwards and all the spaces rightwards and downwards.

Then fill the spaces from left to right and top to bottom, and continue play by eliminating any pairs that are next to each other. Always eliminate everything possible before closing up.

Keep going. You win if you succeed in eliminating all the cards.

The game does not often come out. The only chance you have to exercise skill lies in choosing which pair to eliminate when three or four of the same rank are next to one another.

Triplets

Deal all cards face up in sixteen 'fans' (overlapping groups) of three and two fans of two. Keep eliminating any three uncovered cards in numerical order, regardless of suit, and counting circularly (e.g. K, A, 2 is acceptable). You win by getting all eliminated, apart from the odd one left over. For additional skill, you might remove an odd card from the opening layout before starting play.

Fourteens

Deal 25 cards face up in five rows of five as for **Monte Carlo**.

Eliminate any two cards in the same row or column if they total fourteen. For this purpose count Jack 11, Queen 12 and King 13.

After each elimination, fill the spaces with the next two cards from stock.

When no cards remain in stock and no further eliminations can be made, fill spaces from left to right in the top row with cards taken from right to left in the bottom row, and continue play.

If you succeed in eliminating all the cards you have won the game.

Fourteen Out

An old game, and obvious forerunner of **Fourteens**.

Deal twelve cards face up in a row, then twelve more across and overlapping them, followed by two more rows. Deal the last four cards to the ends of the first four columns.

Eliminate any pair of uncovered cards which total fourteen, counting Jack 11, Queen 12 and King 13. Keep going until you either can go no further or win by eliminating all 52 cards.

Gay Gordons

There is a tradition of naming patience games after Old Tyme dances, and this one of my invention follows that venerable practice. It will be recognised as related to the preceding games.

Deal ten cards face up in a row, then ten more across and overlapping them, and so on until you have five rows of ten. The last two are placed one atop the other as a reserve.

Examine the ten columns. If any contains exactly three Jacks, exchange one of them for the top card of the reserve (or, if that also is a Jack, for the other reserve card.)

Eliminate pairs of uncovered cards if they are numerals and total 11 (e.g. Ace + Ten). Pair off and eliminate any King and Queen of different suits (to avoid inbreeding). Jacks – or 'Gordons' – pair off together.

You win by eliminating all 52 cards.

Gaps (Spaces)

This unusual but delightful game, affording some opportunity for skilful play, is easier to follow with a pack of cards than it may sound from just reading the words.

Deal all cards face up in four rows of thirteen, with no overlapping. Remove the Aces so as to leave four gaps. Your aim is to rearrange the cards in such a way that each row becomes a suit-sequence running from Two (left) to King (right). Play as follows.

Fill each gap with a card which continues the suit-sequence upwards from the left. For example, if there is a gap to the right of ♣7, fill it with ♣8. This creates new gaps, of course, which you then fill in the same way.

A gap to the right of a King obviously cannot be filled. A gap made at the extreme left of a row must be immediately filled with any Two. The choice of Two determines which suit-sequence is to be formed in that row, and the decision, once made, must stand.

Keep going until stuck, which happens when there is a gap to the right of every King. Then gather up all the cards which do not yet form part of a suit-sequence beginning with a Two. Shuffle them thoroughly and deal them back into the layout, starting at the top row and dealing face up from left to right. In each row, do not start immediately to the right of a sequence, but leave a gap between the

Gaps   How a game might look when you have played as far as you can on the first deal. You have just gathered up the non-aligned cards and will start redealing from the positions marked with a cross.

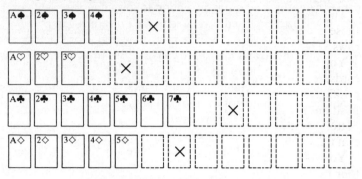

end of the sequence and the first new card dealt. If a row does not yet begin with a Two, leave a gap where the Two will go and start dealing immediately to the right of it.

Some writers allow you two such redeals and some only one. As it is rather fun to play, I suggest you have as many redeals as it takes and for each one donate a pound to charity. Don't worry – it's bound to come out eventually!

Spaces and Aces

Robert Harbin invented this variation on **Gaps**. Deal four rows of thirteen, as above. Take the Aces and place each one to the extreme left of a row. (Choose carefully, as you cannot change them later.) This leaves four gaps as before, but now you are trying to complete four thirteen-card suit sequences from Ace (left) to King (right). Fill any gap with a higher card of the same suit as the card to the left of the gap. (It need not be in sequence.) This gives you more choice of play, and hence more opportunity for skill; but you still cannot play anything to the right of a King, and there is no redeal.

Maze

Maze is a more advanced version of **Gaps**. I suggest you leave it until you have tried **Gaps**, as **Maze** is less easy to follow from the printed page if you are not already experienced at this type of patience.

Deal all the cards face up into six rows, without overlapping. There should be nine cards in the first four rows and eight in the last two. Remove the Aces, which have no further part to play.

This leaves a layout of 54 positions, six of which are gaps, i.e. those left by the removal of Aces plus one at the end of the last two rows.

You must now regard this layout as consisting of a single line of cards, reading from top left to bottom right like lines in a book. A position at the extreme right of a row is followed immediately by the position at the extreme left of the next row. Furthermore, the bottom right-hand gap is consecutive with the top left-hand gap, so that the whole run of 54 positions forms a closed loop.

Your object is to get the cards arranged in such a way as to form four twelve-card suit-sequences, each running from Two to King reading bookwise from left to right and top to bottom. Each King will be followed by the Two to the next suit. It doesn't matter what order the four suits come in, nor does it matter where the gaps occur, nor even does it matter which card happens to occupy the top left position – just so long as they all finish up in suit and sequence all the way along the line.

Play by filling a gap with a card which continues the suit-sequence with the card on either side of it. For example, into a gap flanked by ◇4 on the left and ♠Q on the right you may transfer either ◇5 or ♠J. To the right of a King you may put any Two of a different suit; but you may not play a King to the left of a Two (unless it also matches a Queen to its left).

Where two or more gaps fall together, only those with a card on one side can be filled, and then only with one possible card.

Auld Lang Syne

You could hardly wish for a simpler explanation of why Patience is so called than that provided by **Auld Lang Syne**, which requires much patience but very little thought.

Take out the Aces and lay them in a row at the top of the board. Your aim is to build a complete suit-sequence up to the King on each one, as and when (and if!) the intervening cards become available.

Below the Aces, deal four cards face up in a row. If any are Twos, build them on their respective Aces but do not yet fill the gap(s) they leave.

Deal another row of four across the first, then pause and see if any of them can be built – a Two on an Ace, a Three on a Two, and so on.

Continue dealing four in a row in the same way, pausing each time to build any that will fit. Only the top (uncovered) card of a row is available for building, but building one frees the card below for the same purpose.

Eventually, the game will either 'come out' with all the cards arranged in four suit-sequences, or – far more frequently – will block. If you like dispiriting games such as this, you may wish to try the harder version called **Tam O'Shanter**, which is almost the same except that you don't take the Aces out first but have to wait until they turn up in the deal of their own accord.

You may find yourself inviting this game to be forgot and never brought to mind!

Cat's Cradle

This unusual patience was invented by Michael Bourne of Leeds, to whom I am grateful for permission to publish it for the first time.

Deal sixteen cards face up in four rows of four, with no over-lapping. Your aim is to get the remaining 36 cards entered into this layout in accordance with the following rules of play.

A card may be taken and placed on top of another card which is one rank higher and of opposite colour (e.g. red Three on black Four, black King on red Ace, etc.), but only if both cards lie in the same line – whether horizontally, vertically or diagonally.

Having made as many shifts as you can in this way, fill the spaces bookwise from top left to bottom right with the next cards from stock, then pause and continue play as before.

Keep doing this until either you succeed in getting all cards into play or the game blocks, in which case you have lost.

The game fails more often than not, but offers many opportunities for advance planning and skilful play, and should not be lightly abandoned. Wherever you have a choice of moves you

Cat's Cradle You won't often get a situation offering as many lines of play as this, but be warned – they're easy to miss if you do. The dotted outline shows where ◇7 has been moved on to ♣8. The best sequence of moves would then be: ♡J on ♠Q, ♡9 on ♠10, ♣8 and ◇7 on ♡9, ♣6 on ♡7, ◇5 on ♣6.

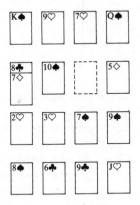

should pay close attention to the alternative consequences before committing yourself. In fact, you may need to play the game several times before acquiring the knack of spotting what the alternatives are, as they are often easily overlooked.

I feel that so interesting and original a game should offer you rather better chances of success, and venture to offer the following 'grace'.

If, after a fresh deal, no move can be made from the new position, turn the next card from stock and see if it can be placed anywhere on the layout on a card next higher in rank and of opposite colour. This occasionally allows moves to be made resulting in the creation of another space; but if it does not do so immediately then the game is lost.

A more certain way of improving the chances of success is to vary the rule of redealing, as follows.

Gaps need not be filled in the prescribed order. Instead, turn cards from stock one by one and consider carefully in which gap to position each one before turning the next. However, having once turned a card you may not change the position of the previous one, and you may not start transferring cards until all gaps have been filled.

Poker Patience

Deal 25 cards face up to the table in the form of a 5 × 5 square, pausing after each card to consider where best to place it. Having once placed a card, you may not later change its relative position.

Your aim is to score as high as possible for all the Poker combinations that can be made from the finished square. Since a Poker hand by definition consists of five cards, there will be ten such hands, represented by the five rows and the five columns.

The scores are:

Straight Flush = 30 (all in suit and sequence)
Fours   = 16 (four of the same rank plus an odd card)
Straight   = 12 (all in sequence but not of one suit)
Full House   = 10 (three of one rank plus a pair)
Threes   = 6 (three of one rank and two odd cards)
Flush   = 5 (all one suit but not in sequence)
Two Pair   = 3 (pair of one rank, pair of another, one odd)
One Pair   = 1 (pair of one rank, three odd)

In making a sequence, Ace may count either low (Ace to Five) or high (Ten to Ace), but not both at once (e.g. not Q, K, A, 2, 3). Count a 'win' if you score 75 or more points.

Pontoon Patience

If Poker Patience, why not also one for Pontoon players? Here is my way of doing it.

Deal cards face up, adding their face values together as you go. Court cards count 10 each and Aces either 1 or 11 as you prefer. So, for example, you might begin as follows:

◇6 = 'six'
♠2 = 'eight'
♣A = 'nine or nineteen' . . .

Stop dealing when the hand totals at least 11 or more than 21. A hand counting over 21 is 'bust' and is placed on the left or losing side of the board. A hand worth from 12 to 21 is 'good' and is placed on the right or winning side of the board. If the last hand is worth less than 12 it is 'bad'. Your aim is to finish with no bad hands and not more than 21 good ones.

Poker Patience This completed square demonstrates every type of Poker hand and produces a score of 83. The individual scores are:

Top row:	Straight Flush = 30
2nd row:	Four of a kind = 16
3rd row:	Full house = 10
4th row:	Flush = 5
5th row:	Straight = 12
Left col:	Threes = 6
2nd col:	Two Pair = 3
3rd col:	One Pair = 1
4th col:	Nothing = 0
5th col:	Nothing = 0

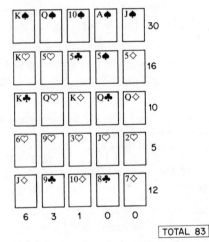

Cribbage Patience

I suppose this can best be described as **Poker Patience** for cribbage players. Several versions have been devised, of which this one strikes me as best.

Deal sixteen cards face up in the form of a 4 × 4 square, pausing after each card to determine the best place to put it. Deal the seventeenth card face up to one side as the 'starter'. Again, having once placed a card, you may not later change its relative position.

Each row and each column of the square is now valued in

accordance with principle of five-card Cribbage hands, with the starter being counted as its fifth card.

The scores are:

Fifteen = 2 points (i.e. two cards totalling 15, counting Ace 1 and court cards 10 each)

Pair = 2 (two of the same rank)

Prial = 6 (three of the same rank)

Double pair royal = 12 (four of the same rank)

Run = 1 per card (three or more in numerical sequence, for which purpose Ace counts as 'one' only)

Flush = 4 or 5 (all cards in the row being of the same suit = 4, plus 1 if the starter is also of that suit).

Score also 'two for his heels' if the starter is a Jack, or 'one for his nob' if your square includes the Jack of the same suit as the starter.

Cribbage Patience   With ♣K as the starter and hence the fifth card in each hand, the individual scores are:

Top row: 2 for K+5, 2 for 8+6+A, 5 for the flush = 9
2nd row: 4 for the flush = 4
3rd row: four lots of 2 for fifteen (each King with each Five), two pairs = 12
4th row: prial of Nines = 6, +1 for his nob = 7
Left col: three lots of 2 for fifteen, 2 for the pair = 8
2nd col: 2 for K+5, 2 for 8+2+5 = 4
3rd col: 2 for 7+8, 3 for the run = 5
4th col: three lots of 2 for fifteen and 2 for the pair = 8

That makes 57, including 1 for his nob (♣J). Not a winning total.

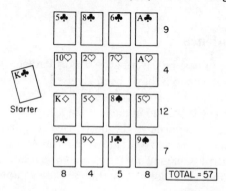

Count a 'win' for scoring 61 or more points in all.

Note: Any card in a Cribbage hand may count as part of more than one combination at the same time. For example, the combination A-3-3-2-6 scores 2 for the Fifteen, plus 3 each for the two runs, plus 2 for the pair, total 10 points.

Quadrille

Several patience games are named after dances. This early example compensates in attractiveness for what it lacks in mental challenge.

Arrange four Queens decoratively in the middle and surround them with all the Fives and Sixes. Aim to build the Sixes up in suit to the Jacks, and the Fives down in suit to the Kings. Turn cards from stock and build them if possible or else discard them face up to a single wastepile, from which you can always play the top card if it fits. You may redeal the wastepile three times, making four deals in all. This is not always enough to bring the game out.

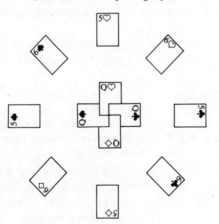

Quadrille   The opening layout.

Labyrinth

Labyrinth, to which I can find no reference earlier than 1905, must have been invented by someone who liked the simplicity of **Auld**

Lang Syne but wanted something a little more cooperative, as it has a similar mode of play but comes out far more often. It requires care and concentration, but offers no opportunity for the exercise of skill.

Take out the four Aces and put them in a row at the top of the board. The aim is to build them in suit and sequence up to their Kings.

From the shuffled pack, deal the first eight cards face up in a row. If any are Twos, build them on their Aces and refill the gaps they leave. Keep building any Twos, Threes, etc. if they appear, and so on, until you have a row of eight which cannot be built on any of the suit piles.

Now deal another row of eight across the first row, overlapping so that all are visible. Build on the suit piles any of the sixteen cards that will fit, as far as you can, but do not fill the gaps they leave.

Continue the game by always dealing a row of eight across the previous row, then playing off any cards from the top or bottom row that can be built on the suit piles. You cannot take a card from an intermediate row until it has been cleared by removal of all the cards above or below it in the same column. Do not fill any gaps that may be left, but wait for them to be filled automatically by the next deal of eight.

When you run out of cards, continue building from the tops and bottoms of columns, until the game either comes out or blocks.

Demon (Canfield)

This legendary patience remains popular as a competitive family game under the title **Racing Demon** or **Pounce**. In America, it was retitled **Canfield** after the owner of a Saratoga gambling saloon, who hit upon the ingenious notion of selling clients a pack of cards for a round of **Demon**, and promising to repay them so much for each card they managed to play from the 'demon' pile before the game blocked. Needless to say, success offered welcome reward. Equally needless to say, the game rarely gets very far before it blocks! (In America, **Demon** is known as **Canfield**. But **Canfield**, in Britain, is a game known to the Americans as **Klondike**. It seems advisable, therefore, to stick to the original names **Demon** and **Klondike**, and to drop the ambiguous **Canfield**.)

Demon The first diagram shows the start of a game, where the ♣8 can be founded immediately, the second a stage in the same game when the wastepile has been turned for the first time. A long sequence of moves can be made as follows: ◇K-♣A, ♠Q-◇K, ♣J to space left by ♠Q, ♣2-♡3, ♠10-♠9, ♡10-♣J, ♠J-♠10, ♠Q-♠J. (Despite this promising patch, the game blocked with four cards left in the Demon.)

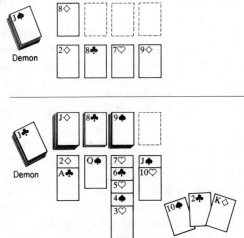

Start of game
Game in progress

As illustrated, start by dealing a pile of thirteen cards face down and turning the top card face up. This packet is the Demon itself, as you will see when it comes to claim you for its own.

Deal the next card face up at the top of the board to act as the first foundation card, then four cards face up in a row beneath it. These four make the first row of the tableau. The aim is twofold. One is to build the foundation card up in suit and sequence until it contains thirteen cards, turning the corner from Ace to King as necessary. The other is to release the other three cards of the same rank as the first foundation card, as and when they become available, and to build them up in the same way.

To play, turn cards from the stock in sweeps of three at a time and lay them face up on a single wastepile. (When fewer than three remain, of course, you 'sweep' whatever is left.) You may spread them so that all are visible, but may only use them as they come – that is, from the top of the wastepile downwards. After each sweep do as many of the following things as can and should be done:

Play any available card to a suit pile if it is the next one up in suit and sequence, or if it is one of the required foundations. Cards counting as 'available' are the top of the wastepile, an uncovered card in the tableau, and the top of the Demon.

When the Demon card is taken, the one below it is turned face up. If and when all the Demon cards are played off, the space they leave may be filled with any available card as a temporary reserve, but only one at a time.

Any available card which cannot be built on a suit pile may, if possible, be packed on an exposed card in the tableau. Packing goes in descending sequence and alternating colour (red Two on black Three, black Ace on red Two, red King on black Ace, etc.). So long as this rule is observed, a single exposed card, or any sequence of properly packed cards, may be transferred from one column of the tableau to another.

The four packed columns of the tableau are spread towards you so that all cards are visible. If a column is completely emptied, the vacancy must be filled at once with the top card of the Demon, or, if it is empty, with that of the wastepile.

When you run out of cards, turn the wastepile over and start redealing in sweeps of three as before. Keep playing and redealing until the game comes out or blocks.

Note: You may wonder why cards are to be swept off in threes rather than one at a time, and whether this makes any difference. The answer is that it does, depending on whether the stock is held face down or face up.

Here's why. Suppose you have ten cards in stock. With the stock face down, you deal them off in threes, making available the 1st, 4th, 7th and 10th from the top. None of these fits, so you turn the wastepile over and repeat the process. Again, you turn up cards 1, 4, 7 and 10. Obviously, the game is lost, as you will keep turning up the same unplayable cards.

If you turned them up one at a time, then you would have ten chances of playing a card as opposed to only four, making the game more likely to succeed.

What happens if you deal in threes, but hold the stock face up? The cards available to you first time round are, as before, 1, 4, 7 and 10. Now pick the wastepile up and deal off in threes again, but *without* turning them upside down. This time, the available cards are 10, 9, 6, 3. (Try it.) Next time round, you get 3, 2, 5, 8. Within three deals, all ten cards have become individually available, just as if you had dealt them one at a time – unless, of course, the number in stock is a multiple of three.

It follows that the game comes out more often if the cards are held face up and swept off in threes, and considerably more often if they are taken in ones, whether held up or down.

Duchess

Duchess, also called **Glenwood**, was invented by Morehead and Mott-Smith. It is a more elegant extension of **Demon**, offering rather more choice of play. In some respects it resembles the splendid two-pack game known as **Terrace** or **Queen of Italy**.

Deal twelve cards face up at the top of the board in four fans of three. These form a reserve. Leave room immediately below them for a row of four cards to act as foundations. Below that, deal four cards face up to start the tableau.

Examine the reserve, and take one of the four exposed cards down as the first foundation. The choice of card for first base is obviously important. Your object is to build this up in suit and sequence until it contains thirteen cards, turning the corner from King to Ace as necessary. You will also aim to release the other three cards of the same rank as and when they become available, put them in the foundation row and similarly build them up into complete suit sequences.

Turn cards from stock one by one. Build them on the suit piles if possible, or pack them on cards of the tableau in descending sequence and alternating colour (as in **Demon**), or else discard them face up to a single wastepile.

The exposed card of each fan in the reserve is available for building or packing. No card may be played to the reserve.

Within the tableau, exposed cards, or sequences of properly packed cards, may be moved to other columns provided that the join follows the rule. A space made in the tableau must be filled with any exposed card from the reserve, or, if none are left, from the top of the wastepile.

The top card of the wastepile may be built or packed whenever possible. The wastepile may be turned and redealt once only.

Sultan (1)

There are two **Sultans**, of which the two-pack version is probably better known. Both are typical of their age, with pictorial layouts – *divan* here has the sense of 'harem' – and a title which reflects a characteristically Victorian love-affair with the 'mysterious east'.

Start by placing ♡K at the centre of an upright cross, surrounded by the other three Kings and ♡A. (See diagram.) Shuffle the remaining cards thoroughly and deal the next four, face up, one to each corner. These corners make up the 'divan'.

Leaving ♡K undisturbed in the middle, aim to build the ♡A and other three Kings up in suit and sequence to their respective Queens, so that you finish with a picture of the sultan (♡K) surrounded by his consorts. Each King, of course, is covered by the Ace as and when it appears, followed by Two, Three and so on.

Turn cards from the stock one by one and consider where each may be placed. It may go on one of the suit piles if it is the next one up. Or it may be placed on one of the divan cards provided that it

Sultan *Above.* Opening layout. *Below.* End product (if successful).

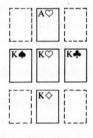

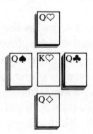

forms a descending sequence regardless of suit – e.g. a Five can be placed on any Six. Failing either, play it face up to a single wastepile.

At any moment, the top card of a corner pile may be played to a suit pile, or the top card of the wastepile to a suit pile or divan corner, provided that it accords with the rules above. When a corner of the divan is emptied, it may be filled with the top card of the stock or of the wastepile, but not with any other.

If, as is likely, you run out of cards before completing the pattern, you may turn the wastepile over and use it as a new stock. But it may only be turned and used once, for if you go on redealing long enough the game is bound to come out eventually.

Czarina

Czarina, also called **Four Seasons**, **Vanishing Cross**, **Corners**, etc., is technically almost identical to **Sultan**.

Deal five cards face up in an upright cross and a sixth in one of the corners. The sixth forms the foundation of a pile which is to be built up in suit and sequence until it contains thirteen cards, (e.g. if it is a Six, the sequence will run 7-K followed by A-5). As and when the other three cards of the same rank appear, they will be placed in the other corners and similarly built into thirteen-card suit sequences.

Turn cards from stock and build them on the suit piles if they fit, or pack them on cross cards in descending sequence regardless of suit (as in **Sultan**, opposite), or else discard them face up to a single wastepile. You may, at any time, build from an exposed cross card to a corner, or place the top waste card wherever it properly fits. A space made in the arms of the cross may be filled with any available card.

Unlike **Sultan**, there is no redeal of the wastepile. This is because it would almost certainly come out on the second round, leaving you with no sense of achievement. As it stands, however, the odds are against success.

Rather than deal the first foundation at random, you may pick out an Ace and build all suit sequences from Ace to King. This version of the game is called **Little Windmill**.

Czarina (and Florentine)   Five cards form the arms of the cross, the sixth goes top left as the first foundation. As it is a Six here, so the other corners will be filled with Sixes when they appear, and all are to be built in suit and sequence to the Fives – by which time the 'cross' will have disappeared (whence the alternative title, **Vanishing Cross**). **Florentine** starts and ends the same, but the centre card – in this instance ♣2 – may not be packed upon.

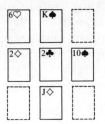

Florentine

This is practically identical to **Czarina**, though the one differing rule gives it a distinctive flavour.

Start as described above. The difference in play is that the centre card remains single – nothing may be placed on it. It may, when possible, be built on a suit pile, but not moved anywhere else. The space it leaves, or any other space made in the cross, may then be filled with a card from stock or from the wastepile.

You are allowed one redeal of the wastepile.

I should mention that old books vary in their accounts of the game, and that the rules given here are based on my own experience of it.

Propeller (Windmill)

This extension of the pictorial cross theme is more often called **Windmill**, though **Propeller** is preferable to avoid confusion with **Little Windmill** (a form of **Czarina**, page 23) and the better-known and – I think – better game played with a double pack (see page 56).

Place the four Aces face up in a central pile. These are for pictorial effect only, having no active role to play.

Regarding these as the cone of the propeller, deal the next eight cards face up in such a way as to form four two-card 'blades' radiating outwards at right-angles to one another.

Propeller *Above*. Opening layout, with four Aces in the middle. Twos are founded in diagonal corners when possible, and built up to Kings. *Below*. End product, if successful.

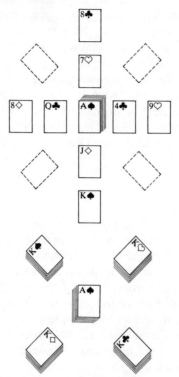

Deal cards one by one from the top of the stock and consider what to do with them. Any Two, when it appears, is to be placed in an angle between two blades. It acts as a foundation card, on which you are to build a sequence of cards – regardless of suit – up to the King.

If a turned card is not a Two or cannot be fitted onto a sequence, it must be discarded face up to a single wastepile. At any time, the top card of the wastepile may be added to a sequence if it fits.

A card from one of the blades may also be added to a sequence whenever possible. The gap it leaves may then be filled with any exposed card, or with the next card turned from stock.

Cards in the four blades may not be packed upon, and there is no redeal of the wastepile.

Note: This patience may lull you into a false sense of security. I estimate that it would always come out the second time round if you were allowed to redeal the wastepile (which I suppose explains why you are not!). It often *looks* as if it will come out the first time, but has a habit of blocking with only a few cards to go. If the cards get shuffled into a 'wrong' order there is no way of winning by skilful play – but you can always overcome unhelpful shuffles by playing very carefully. In practice this means pausing when you find a gap in the blades, and considering whether to fill it from the stock or the wastepile. To this end, you are allowed to spread the waste cards in order to see how many cards you might be able to whittle away – if a lot, you should seize that chance. Otherwise, consider playing from stock.

Golf

Golf, or **One Foundation**, is one of several games with a distinctive feature. Instead of building all the cards into four separate suit piles, your aim here is to build them all into a single pile of 52 cards – so both titles are nicely appropriate.

Deal seven cards face up in a row, then another row of seven overlapping the first, and so on until you have 35 cards out in five rows of seven. Regard the result as seven columns of five.

Deal the next card face up as a base. Your object is to get the rest of the cards built on it in a pile.

Any card from the bottom of a column may be built, provided that it is one rank higher or lower than the top of the pile, regardless of suit. For example, if the top of the pile is a Ten you can play any Jack or Nine from amongst the seven exposed cards. Ace and King are not consecutive – on an Ace you can build only a Two, on a King only a Queen.

Play as far as you can (and wish) from the bottom of the columns. When stuck, deal the next card from stock face up to the pile in order to set it going again. (It doesn't have to be consecutive.)

When a column is emptied, it is not refilled. When there are no cards left in stock, you can only play from the columns. If you do not clear them all out, the number of unplayed cards left is your 'handicap' for the round.

Note: Although the chances are against success, the rules are nicely balanced to produce interesting results. If, for example, you allowed Aces and Kings to be playable on one another, the game would come out too often to be challenging. A reasonable degree of skill is required in deciding which of alternative cards to play from the columns when you have a choice, and when to avoid playing from them even if you can. The game is more subtle than it appears at first sight.

Sir Tommy

Sir Tommy shares with **Grandfather** the reputation of being the oldest of all patience games. Whether that reputation is well founded I cannot say; but as it is technically one of the simplest it may well be true.

It is the first of several games based on a theme affording significant opportunities for skill, of which I think **Strategy** (see page 29) is by far the best. No matter how cleverly you play, I think you will find **Sir Tommy** getting the better of you nine times out of ten – if not more.

Turn cards from stock one by one. Any Ace goes at the top of the board as a base card. Your aim is to build on these bases four piles of thirteen cards each, running from Ace to King regardless of suit.

If the turned card is not an Ace and cannot be built on a sequence, play it face up to any one of four wastepiles. The cards of a wastepile may be spread towards you so that all are visible.

At any time, you may play the last card of a wastepile to a sequence if it fits. You may always look at the next card of stock before deciding whether or not to play from a wastepile. There is no redeal of the wastepiles.

Note: The skill lies in deciding which wastepile to play to, and whether or not to build from one as soon as you can. You can easily vary the details of this simple structure to adjust the average success rate to any desired level. For example, the chances are increased by increasing the number of wastepiles that may be formed, and reduced by requiring the sequences to be built up in suit.

Missing Link

Also known as **Blind Patience** or **Mystery**, here is a variation on **Sir Tommy** which is more likely to be brought to a successful conclusion. The Victorian origin of this species is betrayed by its more apt title, which, being no longer topical, may require elucidation. The original 'missing link' was a hypothetical creature midway between man and the common ancestor of man and ape, whose fossil, if found, would supposedly prove the physical descent of humanity from the rest of the animal kingdom. It always was a more popular than scientific concept, and if we hear little of it now it is probably because more missing links have since been found than anyone knows what to do with.

Cut the pack and deal the top card of the bottom half face down to one side. This card is the 'missing link'.

Turn cards one at a time and either build them if possible or else discard them to any of seven wastepiles. The aim is to found the Aces as and when they appear, and to build them up in sequence to the Kings regardless of suit. The top card of each wastepile is always available for building to an Ace pile.

Keep going until stuck. Then turn up the missing link and see if it can be played to an Ace pile to set the game going again. If so, you have proved the Theory of Evolution. If not, you have lost, as there is no redeal.

Calculation

This variant of **Sir Tommy** is not just more demanding but also more infuriating, as it requires far greater care and attention while offering no greater hope of success.

Lay any Ace, Two, Three and Four in a row at the top of the board – horizontally, so that when built upon they will remain visible as 'indicators' throughout the game. Play as in **Sir Tommy**, turning cards from stock one by one and either building them if they fit or discarding them face up to any of four wastepiles.

As before, the object is to build four thirteen-card sequences from base to King, regardless of suit. In this game, however, a different sequence is followed in each pile, with the intervals between cards shown by the underlying indicators. That is, the Ace pile goes up in ones, the Two pile in twos, the Three in threes and the Four in fours – like this (with T standing for Ten):

```
A 2 3 4 5 6 7 8 9 T J Q K
2 4 6 8 T Q A 3 5 7 9 J K
3 6 9 Q 2 5 8 J A 4 7 T K
4 8 Q 3 7 J 2 6 T A 5 9 K
```

There is no redeal.

Note: The idea of building sequences in different intervals is common to several patience games, and can really be introduced as a variation on any one you like. It adds to the complexity of the task without increasing the skill factor of forward planning, which I think is more essential to the quality of patience than mere computational difficulty. In this particular case the chances against success are so great anyway that I would have no qualms about increasing the number of wastepiles to at least six.

Divorce

This member of the **Sir Tommy** family follows a similar train of thought to that of **Calculation**, but is more likely to result in a happy ending – appropriately or not, depending on your view of its title.

Turn cards from stock and either play them if possible or else discard them to any of four wastepiles.

As the Aces and Twos appear, set them aside as bases for the building of eight sequence piles. Each pile is to be built in alternating colour and sequence, e.g. (with *r* for red and *b* for black):

```
rA,  b3,  r5,  b7,  r9,  bJ,   rK
b2,  r4,  b6,  r8,  bT,  rQ   (etc.)
```

If successful, you finish with eight piles surmounted by Kings and Queens. There is no redeal.

Strategy

Morehead and Mott-Smith are the composers of this elegant extension of the **Sir Tommy** theme. It has long been one of my favourites.

Turn cards face up one by one and play them to any of eight

wastepiles. An Ace, when it appears, goes at the top of the board as a base. Your eventual aim is to build them up in suit and sequence to their Kings.

As you play, only Aces may be set up. All other cards must be played to the wastepiles, which can be spread towards you in columns so that all are visible. Having exhausted the stock, you now build up the suit sequences by playing off the topmost (exposed) cards of the wastepiles.

Note: All the skill lies in deciding which wastepile to play each card to as it comes, planning ahead to the order in which they will eventually have to be played off again. In other words, the game is won or lost by the time you stop dealing cards, and the play-off is purely automatic.

Whether or not the game *can* be won depends to some extent on the result of the shuffling. It is possible to imagine an order of cards which cannot be got out even with best possible play. Morehead and Mott-Smith seem to have this in mind when they estimate the chances of success at one in five. In practice, however, I usually expect to win at least four in five, and I would guess that only a very small percentage of shuffles will produce an unplayable order of cards.

I suggest the following way of increasing the challenge.

Each time you succeed, reduce the number of wastepiles by one in the next game, so that you play first with eight, then seven, then six and so on. Each time you fail, increase the number by one in the next game. Consider yourself to have won the whole series if you get down to four piles, and to have lost if you fail to bring out a game with eight.

Klondike (Canfield)

Klondike is so well known and widely played that many people know it only as 'Patience', not realising that it has a name of its own and is only one of several hundred different patience games. Actually, it has several names, one of which is **Canfield**, but as this is properly the American title for what we call **Demon** it would be wrong to perpetuate it. Other names include **Chinaman**, **Fascination**, and **Triangle**. The last is the most appropriate, as Klondike is

Klondike *Above.* The opening deal looks very promising. You can found ♡A, build ♡2 on it, move ♣K to the space left by ♡2 and pack ◇Q on ♣K, turning three more cards face up. *Below.* Despite that early promise, this is how the game looked when it blocked at the end of the first deal of the stock. (It still failed after five turns and redeals of the wastepile.)

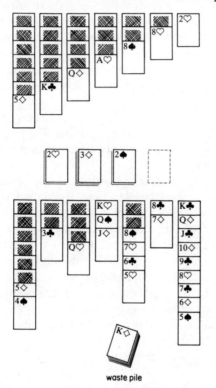

waste pile

the chief one-pack member of a family of games in which the opening layout is (or can be) made in the form of a triangle, the two-pack game being known as **Large Triangle**. The earliest English reference I can find appears in the 1912 series of Mary Whitmore Jones's collection under the title **Small Triangle**. I don't know when it was renamed, but the Klondike gold-rush began in 1896 and it seems reasonable to suppose a Canadian American origin.

Deal seven cards face down in a row. Starting from the same end, deal another card face down on top of the first six, then another on the first five, then likewise four, three, two, and finally one on the first pile in the row. This produces a layout of seven packets of cards ranging in height from seven to one. Turn up the top card of each packet.

If an Ace is visible, place it at the top of the board as a foundation and turn up the card that was lying beneath it. Your aim is to set up all the Aces as and when they become available, and to build them up in suit and sequence to their Kings. If you can do any building of Twos and Threes at this stage (which is most unlikely), do so. Now and throughout the game, whenever a down-card is exposed, turn it face up.

Within the layout you may also pack cards on one another, in descending sequence and alternating colour. For example, you may take an exposed red Nine from one pile and pack it on a black Ten in another, and so on.

Having got as far as you can with the layout, continue play by turning cards from stock one at a time. Build them or pack them if possible, otherwise discard them face up to a single wastepile.

The top card of the wastepile and the exposed card of each column are always available for building or packing. In the layout, a whole sequence of properly packed cards may be moved to another column provided that the join follows the rule, but it is not permitted to take just part of a sequence or a single card (except when building the latter on an Ace pile). If a space is made in the layout by removal of the last card, it may be filled, but only with a King or a sequence headed by a King.

There is no redeal of the wastepile.

Note: As it stands, **Klondike** comes out very rarely – perhaps once in thirty games, according to Morehead and Mott-Smith. I find its popularity so surprising that I have sought to verify the rules by studying every accessible account and experimenting with every variation described. I have to conclude that the rules quoted above are indeed authentic, and that **Klondike** is quite deliberately a hard nut to crack. Perhaps there is a moral to be drawn from its title.

There is a variation in the rules which goes right back to Whitmore Jones, though she herself describes it as a variation rather than as standard. This involves dealing cards from the stock, not one at a time but in sweeps of three (as in **Demon**), and permitting the wastepile to be turned and redealt indefinitely. Dealing in threes is an irrelevance and makes no difference at all, so whether you deal in ones or threes is a matter of taste. But allowing the wastepile to be redealt *does* make a difference: it improves the chances of success from about one in thirty to about one in fifteen!

Another common and well justified variant is to permit packed sequences to be split up where necessary.

My recommendation is that you deal in ones and turn the wastepile as often as you like. What makes Klondike so intractable is the fact that for much of the game a good third of the cards are inaccessible. Against these heavy odds the redealing of the wastepile can hardly be accounted an unfair advantage.

Thumb and Pouch

Play this variation of **Klondike** when you wish to restore your self-confidence. It differs in two respects: firstly, cards in the layout are not packed in alternating colour but in differing suit, e.g. on ♡7 you may pack any Six except of hearts, and secondly a space in the layout may be filled with any available card or sequence, not just a King.

Morehead and Mott-Smith give you three to one against, but I find the game so generous that I suggest Variant Rule 2 be ignored.

Agnes I

Two slightly different versions of **Klondike** share the same name, which I will here call **Agnes I** and **Agnes II** (though I like to think of them as Agnes Sorel and Agnes Bernauer, after historical characters).

Deal seven cards face up in a row, then six across them, then five, and so on down to one. Spread the cards into a triangle (as illustrated). Deal the next card face up as a base. Your aim is to found the other cards of the same rank as the first base, as and when they appear, and to build each base up into a pile of thirteen cards in suit and sequence, turning from King to Ace where necessary.

The exposed card at the end of each column is available for founding or for building on a suit pile, so start by seizing any opportunity to do so. You may also pack cards from one column onto another in descending sequence and matching colour – e.g. a red Seven can take any red Six, and so on. A whole sequence of properly packed cards may be moved if the join follows the rule, but you may not split a sequence for this purpose. A King may be packed on an Ace – unless, of course, either is a base card.

When stuck, deal a card face up to the end of each column (following the same order as in the original deal), then pause and continue play. Keep doing this until you run out of cards – the last two will go on just the first and second columns. You may not interrupt a deal to continue play before it is completed. A gap made by removing the last card of a column is not refilled from the layout, but only by means of the next deal.

There is no redeal. The game rarely succeeds.

Agnes II

This *Agnes* starts outlike the one above and then diverges as follows.

After dealing the first base, deal another row of seven cards beneath the layout. These form a reserve. On the layout, pack cards

Agnes An opening layout for **Agnes II**. (**Agnes I** is the same but without the seven-card reserve.) In both games, ♡J can be founded immediately (followed in **Agnes I** by ♡Q from the reserve), and any space subsequently made in a column is to be filled with a Ten. In **Agnes II** you would continue by playing ♡8 or ◇8 to ♣9; in **Agnes I** by playing ♣9 to ♣T, then ♠8 to ♣9.

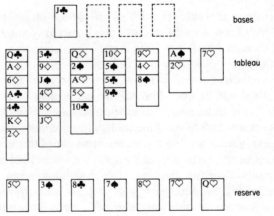

in descending sequence and alternating colour, moving whole (but not part) sequences where appropriate. A space in the columns may be filled with any available card which is one rank lower than that of the base cards.

No packing takes place on the cards of the reserve, but all its uppermost cards are available for packing on the layout or building on the suit piles.

When stuck, cover the reserve with seven more cards dealt from stock. (This is the only way in which gaps in the reserve may be filled.)

Again, the chances are against success.

Will-o'-the-Wisp

This invention of Morehead and Mott-Smith belongs to a family of games which I call 'spiders' – after the most illustrious of that tribe, the two-pack **Spider** which you will find on p. 93. These are games in which the sequences are built up within the tableau, instead of on cards taken out separately and set up as bases. **Will-o'-the-Wisp** is in fact a modification of a game called **Spiderette**, which does not come out often enough to be very attractive.

Deal seven cards in a row face *down*, then seven more across and overlapping them, and finally another seven face *up* to complete the opening tableau. The fourteen down cards will be turned face up as and when they become exposed.

Your aim is to build up four complete suit sequences within the tableau. Each sequence will run from King down to Ace in numerical order, and is to be discarded from the tableau when complete, though not until you find it convenient to throw it out.

Start by packing exposed cards on one another in descending sequence. They need not be in suit to start with, but, as you will need to get them into suit eventually, it is helpful to follow suit whenever possible. You may pack cards singly or in any length of properly packed sequence, and a space made by clearing out a column may be filled with any available card or sequence.

When stuck, fill any gaps in the tableau, deal seven more cards face up across the columns, and continue play. There will only be three cards left on the last deal, and they must go on the first three columns.

There is no redeal.

Scorpion

Another member of the 'spider' family, like **Will-o'-the-Wisp**, this one really has a sting in its tail. It may not come out very often, but gives you plenty of scope for skill.

Deal four cards face down in a row, followed by three more face up. Deal three more rows across and overlapping them, also of four down and three up. Complete the layout with four more rows of seven, dealing them all face up. Spread the last three cards face down in a fan to one side, forming a reserve.

Your aim is to complete four thirteen-card suit sequences within the tableau, each running from King down to Ace. Completed sequences are not discarded from the layout.

You may place on any exposed card in the layout that card which is of the same suit and next lower in rank (e.g. ♡3 goes on ♡4). The card so moved may come from anywhere in the layout, but any and all other cards that may be covering it must also be moved with it as a unit. Nothing may be packed on an Ace.

When a down-card is uncovered, turn it face up.

A space made in the tableau may be filled only with a King, together with any and all cards lying on top of it.

When stuck, deal the three reserve cards face up across the three leftmost columns and continue play.

There is no redeal.

Curds and Whey

A game of my own invention, *Curds and Whey* belongs, as its title may suggest, to the 'spider' family – see also **Will-o'-the-Wisp**, **Scorpion**, and two-pack games headed by **Spider**. It introduces the novel idea of packing cards by rank ('curds') as well as suit ('whey'). I only wish I could add that this novelty increased its chances of coming out. (Incidentally, I am very fond of curds and whey, otherwise known as junket, and am surprised to find that it has practically vanished from the culinary scene. If you want the real thing these days, try health food shops.)

Deal four rows of thirteen cards each, face up, with rows overlapping one another. Your aim is to build four thirteen-card suit sequences within the tableau, each running from King down to Ace.

Exposed cards may be packed on one another in suit and descending sequence, and properly packed sequences of cards may be moved as a whole from column to column provided that the join follows this rule.

Alternatively, the exposed card of a column may be built on any other of the same rank – e.g. any Four on any Four, King on King, etc. – and two or three together can be moved as a unit.

You may build a sequence on a group or a group on a sequence, provided that the join follows the rule. You may, as is sometimes necessary, split a group or sequence and move just part of it. But you may not lift and move a combination of a group and a sequence as one unit.

A space made in the layout may be filled only with a King, together with any sequence or group (but not both) which it may head.

If the game blocks completely you may take the following 'grace' and count half a win for subsequently bringing it out: assuming there is at least one space in the layout, move into it a single exposed card (not a group or a sequence) from the end of any column.

Note: Although the game does block more often than not, it tends to happen late in the game. You need to keep both eyes open and all your wits about you, as a large number of alternative lines of play will be presented for quite a long time. Once the Kings have made their way to the heads of columns, be very reluctant to make any more spaces in the layout than are absolutely necessary.

Bristol

This neat little game by Morehead and Mott-Smith introduces games of the 'Fan' family. A 'fan' is a row of overlapping cards. The 'top' end is the one with the uncovered card. Only uncovered cards are 'available' for moving to other positions.

Bristol Eight fans have been dealt. The ♠K can be moved to below ♡8. The ◇A and ◇2 can be played off and ♣J moved to ♡Q. There are then several alternative moves which can be made.

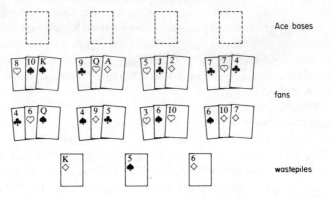

Deal eight three-card fans face up. If you can see a King, move it to the bottom of its fan. (This makes things easier.)

Your aim is to free the Aces and build them up in suit and sequence to the Kings. If any Ace is available, you can start immediately. Otherwise, play as follows.

Deal three cards from stock and use them to start three waste piles. Keep dealing in threes, going across the waste piles in the same order. After each three-card deal, pause and see what can be done.

The top cards of the waste piles are 'available', along with the tops of the fans. Any available card may be built on an Ace pile if it fits. Or it may be built on a fan in descending sequence regardless of suit, e.g. any Ten can be played to a Jack at the top of a fan.

Only one card may be moved at a time. An empty fan is not replaced. There is no redeal.

Not surprisingly, it usually fails.

Fan

This attractive and intelligent patience is so called partly because the whole layout reproduces the shape of a fan, and partly because the cards are dealt in groups that look like little fans.

Deal all the cards face up in sweeps of three at a time. Arrange the seventeen sweeps in the shape of a fan (if you like), with the odd card representing its 'handle' (see diagram). From now on, a 'fan' means any of these eighteen groups, even if it only contains one card.

Your aim is to play the Aces out and build each one up in suit and sequence to its King.

The uncovered card of any fan is 'available'. It may be taken and placed on another in suit and descending sequence, e.g. ♡5 on ♡6, ♡4 on ♡5, etc. Only one may be moved at a time. When an Ace is uncovered, put it to one side for building. Build on the Aces as and when the appropriate cards become available.

When a fan is emptied, its space may be filled with a King (nothing else), provided one is available for the purpose.

As there is no redeal, the game rarely comes out.

Fan, Belle Lucie, Shamrocks   Opening layout.

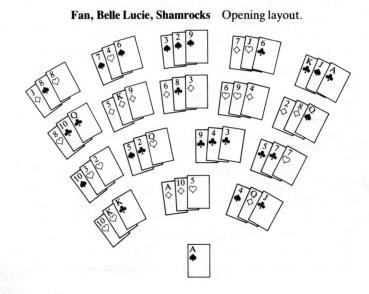

Belle Lucie

This is a version of **Fan** with a greater chance of success, though it still fails more often than not. Play as described above but with these differences.

A space made by emptying a fan may not be refilled. When the game blocks, gather up all the fan-cards (i.e. those not yet built on Ace piles), shuffle them, and deal them out again in fans of three at a time as far as they will go. The last fan may contain only one or two cards, of course.

No more than two such gatherings and redeals are allowed. Obviously, it would come out eventually if you went on redealing often enough.

Note: In both games, you may alternatively deal cards out in sixteen fans of three and two of two. It makes very little difference.

Shamrocks (Three-Card Fan)

This much tougher version of **Fan** has the same opening layout and objective. Start by moving all Kings to the bottom of the fans they are in. Pack exposed cards on one another in ascending or descending sequence regardless of suit (e.g. any Five on any Four or Six).

The hard part is that no fan may ever contain more than three cards at a time. If you cannot make a start because there is no exposed Ace, you may remove any one of the buried Aces to set it going.

Black Hole

A game of my invention, **Black Hole** may be laid out either like **Fan** or (in keeping with the title) as shown below. It will nearly always come out if you play it perfectly, but you have to look a long way ahead for that to happen.

The black hole – a degenerate star which gobbles up everything that comes near it – is represented by the ♠A. Start by placing it in the middle, then deal all the other cards face up around it in seventeen orbiting fans of three cards each.

The top card of each fan is available for building on the central pile. Its removal renders the one below available in its turn.

The object is to finish with all 52 cards built up in the centre. Throughout the game, an available card may be built if it is either one rank above or one rank below the top card of the pile, regardless of suit. For this purpose, Ace and King are consecutive.

Black Hole This one came out. Can you do it?

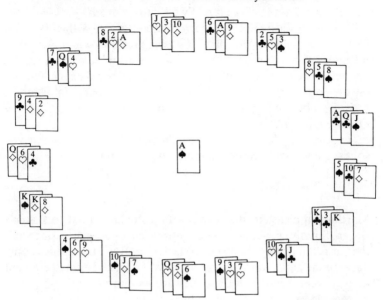

So, for example, it is possible to go K, Q, J, Q, K, A, 2, 3, 2, 3, 4, etc.

Baker's Dozen

This is one of several games which are the intelligent patience-player's delight, to wit, those in which all the cards are dealt face up to start with so as to afford you maximum opportunity for the exercise of skill, which, as you will soon discover, is not the same thing as saying that they will always come out, even with perfect play.

Deal thirteen cards face up in a row, then thirteen more on top of them, followed by a third and a fourth row of thirteen. Spread the cards slightly towards you so that all are visible. What you now have is thirteen columns of four cards each.

Your aim is to extract the Aces, as and when they become available, and build them up in suit and sequence to the Kings. Start by moving any Kings to the buried ends of the columns they occupy – unless you want to make it really hard for yourself.

The card at the open end of each column (the one with nothing on top of it) is 'available' for play. If it is an Ace, place it at the top of the table as a foundation. If it is next up in suit and sequence, build it on the appropriate Ace pile. Otherwise it may be taken and packed on any other available card which is exactly one rank higher, regardless of suit. That is, any Queen goes on any King, Jack on Queen, and so on.

A vacancy made by emptying a column may not be refilled. Even so, the game should come out more often than not.

Martha

Martha is a pleasant little game with a similar format to **Baker's Dozen**. Strictly speaking, it is not entirely an 'open' game, since half the cards are dealt face down to start with. But I think this is only because the game would be far too easy if it lacked a small element of uncertainty, and in any case they are soon turned up.

Remove the Aces and aim to build them up in suit and sequence to the Kings.

Deal a row of twelve cards face down. Across them deal twelve more face up. Follow with twelve face down and twelve face up again. This leaves twelve columns of four, with the end card of each column lying face up. The end cards are 'available' for play. Whenever a face-down card is uncovered, turn it face up.

Available cards may be built on Ace piles if they fit, or packed on one another in descending sequence and alternating colour, e.g. red Queen on black King, etc. Such a sequence may be shifted as a whole to another column provided that the join follows the rule.

A vacancy made by emptying a column may be filled with any one available card (not a sequence).

The chances of success are greatly in your favour.

Beleaguered Castle

Beleaguered Castle, also known as **Sham Battle** or **Laying Siege**, is one of the oldest and simplest patiences of its kind – its kind being those which start off with all cards visible as in **Baker's Dozen** and others on the following pages. The earliest ancestor I can find is **La Forteresse**, described by Lady Cadogan in 1870. The 1890 collection by 'Cavendish' includes the substantially similar **Fort**, though by this time **Beleaguered Castle** had already appeared in the American collection by William Dick.

Remove the four Aces and lay them in a vertical line down the middle of the table. Your object is to build them up in suit and sequence to the Kings.

On each side of each Ace deal six cards face up in a horizontal row, overlapping one another. These eight rows are called 'wings'. At any time, only the end card of each wing – the one which has no other card on top of it – is available for building on an Ace pile or moving to another wing. End cards may be packed on other end cards to form descending sequences regardless of suit, e.g. Queen on King, Jack on Queen, etc. Only one such card may be moved at a time. A vacancy made by emptying a wing may be filled with any available card.

You can expect to succeed once in every two or three games.

Bouquet

This patience, also known as **Flower Garden** or **Parterre**, should be well known to all serious players. It is a game of skill, but does not often come out even with perfect play.

Deal 36 cards face up in six rows of six. Each row may overlap the previous one to save space, and you will naturally regard the finished layout as consisting of columns rather than rows. Hold the remaining sixteen cards in hand. These form the 'bouquet'.

Play to release the Aces and build them up in suit and sequence to their Kings.

The uncovered end card of each column is available for taking as a foundation if it is an Ace, or for building on an Ace pile if it fits. Or it may be packed on the end of another column to form a descending sequence regardless of suit (e.g. any Queen on any King, Jack on Queen, etc.). Only one card may be moved at a time. A vacancy made by emptying a column may be filled with any single available card.

All cards of the bouquet are simultaneously available for building on Ace piles or for packing on the ends of columns if they follow the appropriate rules. Cards of the bouquet are not replaced when taken.

Eight Off

A variant of this under the title **Baker's Game** once formed the subject of an article in Martin Gardner's 'Mathematical Games' department of *Scientific American* (June 1968), thus demonstrating the potential attraction of patience games to mathematicians. Apart from that, it is neither more nor less remarkable than any other of the immediately preceding or following games in which all cards are open to examination before any opening move is made.

Deal eight cards face up in a row. Deal eight more on top of them, and keep repeating the procedure until you have six rows of eight and four cards left over. Spread the cards slightly so that all are visible, and regard the layout as consisting of eight columns of six cards each. Lay the odd four face up to one side, not overlapping, to form a reserve.

Play to release the Aces when possible and build them up in suit and sequence to the Kings.

The uncovered card at the end of each column is 'available', as are all cards of the reserve. Any available card may be taken to start a sequence (if it is an Ace) or to continue one if it is next in succession. An available card may also be packed on the end card of any column to form a descending suit sequence (e.g. ♡Q on ♡K, etc.).

A vacancy made in the layout by emptying a column may be filled only with an available King.

Although the reserve starts off with four cards, it may contain up to eight at any one time. A space in the eight-card reserve may be filled with the exposed card of any column – so that it acts, in other words, as a sort of shunting yard.

Baker's Game

Eight Off usually comes out. In the more challenging version, described by Martin Gardner as **Baker's Game**, the last four cards are dealt to the ends of the first four columns, and the reserve – empty to start with – may contain up to four cards (not eight).

Suit Yourself

A simple little game of my invention, which takes a lot of thought but should come out as often as not – with perfect play.

Deal all the cards face up in overlapping rows of eight, except that the last (seventh) row will contain only four. Regard the result as eight columns.

Your aim is to eliminate all 52 cards from the tableau in the following way.

Throughout play, the exposed card at the near end of each column is 'available'. At each turn, remove three or more available cards which are of the same suit. If more than three of a suit are available you need not take them all, but you may never remove fewer than that number.

This means that you will fail if ever you leave exactly two of each suit available. (If the opening deal turns out this way, you may take any available card and shift it to the opposite end of the column it is in.) You will also fail if, near the end, you leave fewer than three cards of a suit in the tableau.

A space made by emptying a column may be filled with any available card.

Penguin

This game of my invention (which I also call **Beak and Flipper**) belongs to the same series as **Bouquet** and **Eight Off**, in that all cards are visible to start with and you can do a lot of profitable calculation before making the first move.

Deal seven cards face up in a row. The first of these (at top left, if you deal from left to right) is the 'beak'. Deal seven more across them, then seven more again, and so on as far as you can. Each time you turn up a card of the same rank as the beak, place it at the top of the table as a foundation. When you have finished dealing, you will have seven columns of seven cards each, and three foundation cards.

Your object is to release the beak and put it in place as the fourth foundation, and to build all the foundations up into thirteen-card ascending suit-sequences. (For example, if the beak is a Ten, the foundations are all Tens and the sequence runs J, Q, K, A, 2, 3, 4, 5,

Penguin This opening deal was brought to a successful conclusion. It is always possible to release the 'beak' immediately (♡T in this example) by transferring the cards covering it to the flipper, which can hold up to seven cards at a time. But that is not necessarily the best way of starting.

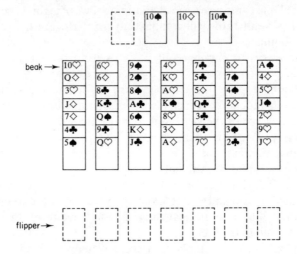

6, 7, 8, 9.) You can, of course, start building on the first three foundations before you get the beak out.

The uncovered end card of each column is available for building on a foundation pile if it continues the sequence, or for packing on the end card in another column in suit and descending sequence, e.g. ♠8 on ♠9, etc. Alternatively, it may be taken and temporarily put to one side in a reserve known as the 'flipper'.

The flipper may contain up to seven cards at any one time. Any card of the flipper may be taken and built on a foundation pile or packed on the end of a column provided that it continues the appropriate sequence.

In the layout, a sequence of properly packed cards may be shifted as a whole to another column provided that the join follows the rule. If a space is made by clearing out a column, it may only be filled with a card which is one rank lower than a foundation (e.g. a Nine if the foundations are Tens), or with a properly packed sequence headed by such a card.

PART TWO
Two-Pack Games

Two-Pack games

Haden

This and **Triple Alliance** are the best of the two-pack elimination games. They should usually come out with perfect play.

Deal twelve cards in a row face up, then twelve more across them, and keep going until you have dealt eight rows and have eight cards left. Spread the last eight face up in a reserve at one side. Your aim is to eliminate all the cards from the layout in accordance with the following rules.

The card at the exposed end of each column is available, as are all eight cards of the reserve. Eliminate all numeral cards in pairs totalling eleven (e.g. Ace + Ten, etc.). Eliminate all court cards in families of three consisting of Jack, Queen, King (regardless of suit).

Although all cards of the reserve are available, they are restricted in use. You may only take from the reserve when you cannot play from the columns, and you may not in one turn discard three court cards from the reserve.

Triple Alliance

The second good eliminator is a two-pack version of **Triplets** (see page 8).

In this game Ace and King are consecutive, so that a sequence may consist, for example, of Q-K-A.

Deal all the cards face up in sixteen fans of six cards and two fans of four. The top card of each fan is available for elimination. Eliminate available cards in sequences of three regardless of suit.

If successful, you will have two cards left over. For additional skill, try to finish with either a pair or two cards in sequence. Or, for sheer torture, start by dealing seventeen fans of six and leaving the last two cards out of play.

Note, by the way, that each run of three must consist of cards taken from three different fans.

Big Wheel (Ferris Wheel, Eighteens)

A numerical game of German origin, whose title reflects the fairground amusement depicted by its suggested layout.

Arrange the Aces in the form of a cross with two placed lengthwise along each arm. Envisage them as the spokes of a big wheel, which will eventually consist of 24 packets of cards arranged in a circle around them.

Beneath the intended wheel, deal a reserve of twelve cards face up. At each turn, eliminate from the layout four cards consisting of one court card plus three *different* numerals together totalling eighteen, e.g. $7 + 6 + 5, 9 + 5 + 4$, etc. Place them in a packet in one of the 24 'wheel' positions with the King, Queen or Jack face up on top.

Fill spaces in the reserve from stock and continue play.

Push-Pin

A squeezy game, **Push-Pin** is the two-pack equivalent of **Accordion** (see page 5). It calls for little skill and rarely comes out, but is rather fun to play.

Deal cards face up in a row from left to right, (unless you are left-handed, in which case either translate the instructions or re-name your hands). Eliminate any card, or any pair of adjacent cards, which is sandwiched between two cards of the same rank or suit. Close the gap up and continue dealing rightwards from the right-hand end.

If three or more cards are sandwiched in this way, they may not be eliminated unless they are all of the same suit, in which case they must *all* go out.

When you have run out of cards and made all the eliminations you can, the only way to set the game going again is to transpose any two cards in the row. To do so once is a 'grace', twice is cheating. You win by whittling the row down to just two adjacent cards.

Weaver's

Weaver's is a shuttling game related to the one-pack **Rondo** (see page 5). It doesn't invite skill and rarely comes out, but it features an unusual and intriguing method of play.

Lay out all eight Kings at the top. Your aim is to build them down in suit and sequence to the Aces.

Deal all the other cards face up in rotation to form twelve piles, counting as you go 'Ace, Two, Three . . .', etc. up to the Queen. If the card you are about to deal matches the next pile, lay it face down to one side and continue from the pile after that.

The finished layout represents a 'loom', and any discards are the 'shuttles'. You are now ready to play.

The uppermost twelve cards are available for building on the King piles. Build as far as you can. When stuck, take a shuttle and play as follows: slip it to the bottom of the pile corresponding to its rank, then take the top card of that pile and slip it to the bottom of the pile corresponding to *its* rank, and so on. (A top card which matches the pile it is on will, of course, be shuttled to the bottom.) Continue 'shuttling' in this way until you take up a card which can be built on a King pile. Build it, then pause to build as many more as you can from the tops of the piles. When stuck, take the next shuttle and repeat the process. You may not, by the way, build a shuttle directly on to a King pile. It must always pass through the loom first.

When you have built as far as you can and run out of shuttles, redeal in the following way. Leaving the King piles alone, gather up the loom piles in reverse order and turn the whole pack upside down without shuffling. Then start again from scratch, except that, this time, you reduce the number of piles built by the number of ranks that have been completely used on the King piles. For example, if all the Queens and Jacks have been built, along with some of the Tens and perhaps a Nine or two, then deal to ten piles instead of twelve.

Precedence

The next few games are variations on a simple theme, some of which are prettier than others. This one comes out just often enough to make it challenging.

Turn cards from the stock one by one and either add them to the pattern described below or discard them face down to a single wastepile.

The pattern starts when the first King appears. Place it at top left, and build on it (as and when the proper cards become available) downwards in sequence to an Ace, regardless of suit. When a Queen appears, either build it on the King or start another column on its right, which is to be built down in sequence until it contains thirteen cards, finishing 2, A, K. Similarly, found a Jack to the right of the Queen, then a Ten, Nine, Eight, Sven and Six, and aim to build them all into thirteen-card downward sequences, regardless of suit and turning from Ace to King where necessary.

The top card of the wastepile is always available for founding or building. The wastepile may be turned and redealt twice, making three deals in all.

Double Dial

One of several games based on the old clockface theme. It does not often come out.

Remove the eight Kings and arrange them decoratively in the centre. (They play no active part in the game.) Take out the following twelve cards and, starting at the one o'clock position, deal them clockwise to form a circle: ♠6, ♡7, ♣8, ◇9, ♠10, ♡J, ♣Q, ◇A, ♠2, ♡3, ♣4, ◇5.

Shuffle the rest and turn them one at a time, building them on the clockface in accordance with the rules below, or else discarding them face up to a single wastepile. On the clockface, build upwards in suit and sequence (passing from Queen to Ace as necessary) until each pile contains eight cards, topped by ♠A at one o'clock, ♡2 at two o'clock, and so on to ♣J at 11 and ◇Q at 12.

The top card of the wastepile may be built if it fits. The wastepile may be turned and redealt twice, making three deals in all.

Double Dial The opening layout.

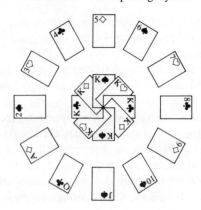

Contradance (Cotillion)

A two-pack version of **Quadrille** (see page 17), this dance-flavoured patience does not often come out.

Take out the Fives and Sixes and arrange them in a circle in pairs of the same suit.

Play, as appropriate cards become available, to build the Sixes up in suit to the Queens and the Fives down in suit to the Kings (King follows Ace).

Turn cards one by one and either build them if they fit or else discard them face down to a single wastepile. The top card of the wastepile is always available for building if it fits.

The wastepile may be redealt twice, making three deals in all.

Marriages (Four Marriages)

Remove one card of each rank from Ace to King, regardless of suit. Shuffle the thirteen together and stack them face up in the middle.

Turn cards from stock one by one, and either play them in accordance with the following rules if possible, or else discard them face up to a single wastepile.

As and when they turn up, found an Ace and a Two of each suit in a suitable eight-card pattern around the centre stack. Your object is to build these up in suit and alternating sequence to the Kings and Queens, i.e. each Ace is followed by 3, 5, 7, 9, J, K, 2, 4, 6, 8, 10, Q and each Two by 4, 6, 8, 10, Q, A, 3, 5, 7, 9, J, K.

Marriages The half above the dotted line shows how Aces and Twos might be arranged around the centre stack; the half below shows how they will appear at the finish, with the centre stack gone.

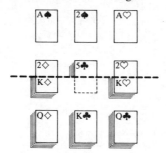

Available for building on these piles are the cards you turn from stock, the top card of the centre stack, and the top card of the wastepile. The wastepile may be turned and used as a new stock twice, giving three deals in all. The chances are against success.

Snail

Snail may be recognised as a disguised version of **Contradance**, and perhaps preferred for its more imaginative layout. It is also more likely to come out (especially after dark).

Remove all Fives, Sixes and Jacks. Lay these out in a spiral starting with the Fives and ending with the Jacks (as illustrated). Deal the next four cards face up in a line under the spiral to form a reserve. Your aim is to build on the Fives downwards in suit to the Kings, and on the Sixes upwards in suit to the Queens (omitting Jacks). The Jacks are not affected, and the four reserve cards will eventually disappear (as if retracted, like the snail's body, into the shell).

Snail Opening layout. When finished, the bottom line will have disappeared and the shell will consist entirely of court cards.

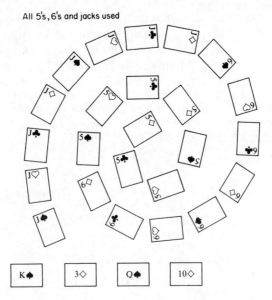

All 5's, 6's and jacks used

Turn cards from stock and build them if possible or else discard them face up to a single wastepile. The top card of the wastepile is available for building if it fits. A reserve card may be built when it fits, and its space immediately filled with the top card of stock or wastepile.

The wastepile may be turned and dealt once more.

Sultan (2)

The two-pack version of a male chauvinist game described earlier. It usually comes out.

Remove eight Kings and ♡A. Arrange them in a 3 × 3 square with one ♡K in the middle to represent the Sultan. Deal the next eight cards face up in two columns of four, one column down each side of the square. These form a reserve called the 'divan'. Your aim is to build a complete suit-sequence up to the Queen on every centre card except the Sultan.

Turn cards from stock and build them if possible or else discard them face up to a single wastepile. The top card of the wastepile is always available for building if it fits. So are all cards of the divan, each of which, when taken, is replaced with the next card from stock or the top card of the wastepile.

The wastepile may be turned and redealt twice, giving three deals in all. Some say the wastepile must be shuffled before re-use, but this rule is absent from the earliest account of the game.

Sultan Opening layout. Each King except the Sultan is followed by A, 2, etc. up to the Queen; ♡A is followed by ♡2, etc. up to the Queen. The finished product depicts a Sultan surrounded by his harem.

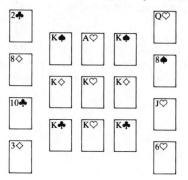

Teenagers

An early version of this rather tough game was called **Matrimony**. I don't like either title. How about **Polyandry** instead?

Set up a ♡J and ♡Q as bases. As and when they become available, set up as bases in line with them two Tens of diamonds, clubs and spades. Play to build eight thirteen-card round-the-corner suit sequences on these bases: the Tens downwards to the Jacks, the Jack downwards to the Queen, and the Queen upwards to the Jack. The final outcome will show ♡Q surrounded by seven admiring Jacks.

Deal sixteen cards face up in two rows of eight. Take any Tens to use as bases and any other cards that may be built. When stuck, deal sixteen more in the same positions, filling spaces or covering unbuilt cards as the case may be, and do any further possible building. Keep going until you run out of cards. (The last deal will be of six only, which go in the first six positions.)

Having run out of cards, continue by taking up each of the unbuilt piles in the same order as dealt. Use each pile as a new stock, dealing the first card to the space it came from and continuing to the right as far as possible. Play again before taking the next pile.

You win if you succeed in getting it out before or by the time you have dealt the sixteenth pile. It doesn't often come out.

Teenagers Eight bases in the top row are completed as the Tens become available. You can start by founding ♠10 and building ♠9 on it. On ♡Q you can build the King and Ace, while ♡10 goes on ♡J.

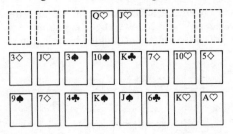

Windmill

A classic game with an apt pictorial theme, **Windmill** is worth replaying several times until you manage to bring it to a successful conclusion.

Windmill   *Above.* An opening layout. A start can be made by playing the King to one of the positions marked with dotted lines. The Queen can be built on the King and the Two on the central Ace, leaving two gaps to be filled from stock. The central Ace is built upwards into a 52-card pile, each King downwards into one of thirteen cards. *Below.* The end product.

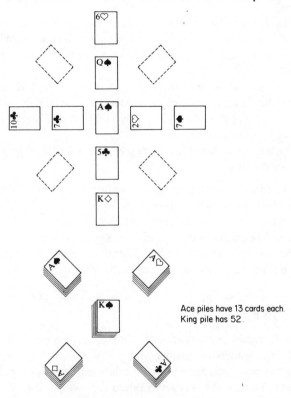

Ace piles have 13 cards each.
King pile has 52.

Deal an Ace to the centre, representing the windshaft, and the next eight cards around it with two radiating from each edge of the Ace, representing the sails (see diagram). As and when the first four Kings appear, place each one between two sails, radiating diagonally from a corner of the central Ace-pile. If there is a King in the opening layout, put it in position at once and refill the space it leaves.

Turn cards from stock and build them in accordance with the rules below, if possible, or else discard them face up to a single wastepile.

All building takes place regardless of suit. On the central Ace, build upwards (i.e. from Two to King, followed by another Ace, etc.) until you have built 52 cards in four complete sequences ending with a King. On each corner King, build downwards to an Ace and then stop.

Available for building are the top card of stock, the top card of the wastepile, and each of eight cards in the sails. When a card is taken from a sail, replace it immediately with the top card of stock or wastepile.

You are also allowed to transfer the top card of any King pile to the top of the Ace pile, or vice versa, if it continues the sequence and you think it helpful. But you may not move a base King or the Ace dealt originally to the centre.

As there is no redeal of the wastepile, it is essential to play from it whenever possible.

Note: It will be seen that in course of play the sails of the windmill are transformed from the cross of St George position (+), which millers used as a sign of distress or mourning, to that of St Andrew (X), denoting a mill at rest or in disuse. The St George cross, known as 'Miller's Pride', would also be adopted 'for luck' for a short while before milling began at the start of each working day.

Wheat-Ear

A natural successor to **Windmill**, with about the same chances of success – i.e. somewhat against you.

Deal twenty cards face up in overlapping V-shaped pairs (see diagram). These form a reserve called the 'wheat-ear'. Deal nine more cards face up. Four of these go down each side of the wheat-ear in two side reserves, the last is a base card. Your aim is to release the other seven cards of the same rank as the first base, and to build them all up into thirteen-card suit-sequences, turning from King to Ace as necessary.

Turn cards from stock and build them if possible or else discard them face up to a single wastepile, whose top card always remains available for building. Also available for building are the eight cards of the side reserves, and the two cards at the exposed (lowest) end of the wheat-ear. When a side reserve card is taken, it is replaced from

Wheat-Ear (and Pigtail)   Both games start with a central reserve of twenty plaited cards, two side reserves of four cards each, and a first base. Pigtail has, in addition, four corner reserve cards dealt to the outlined spaces marked 'C'.

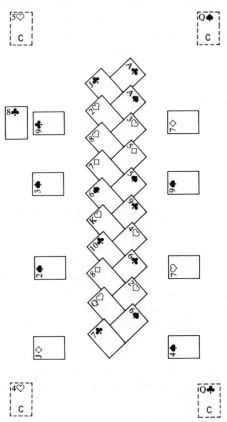

the top of stock or wastepile. Cards from the wheat-ear are not replaced when taken.

The wastepile may be turned and redealt once only.

Pigtail

This is a more often successful variant of **Wheat-Ear** and is also known as **Plait**.

The opening layout, objective and method of play are as already described but with the following differences.

Deal four more cards to start 'corner reserves' shown with a dotted line in the diagram. From the central reserve, here known as the pigtail, only the very last (uncovered) card may be taken. It may be built on one of the base piles, or used to fill a space left in a corner reserve. Corner reserve cards may only be replaced from the pigtail. Side reserves may be filled only from stock or wastepile.

The wastepile may be turned and redealt three times, giving four rounds of play.

Note: A game of similar design but more elaborate play is **Backbone**, page 76.

Diamond

This may be seen as a forerunner of the delightful **Quilt**, and should come out as often as not.

Deal 41 cards face up in a diamond shape, with nine in the middle row, seven each in a row above and below it, five in each next row, three in the next, and one at top and bottom. This forms a reserve. Your aim is to found the Aces as they become available and to build each up in suit and sequence to the King.

Turn cards from stock three at a time and found or build them if possible or else discard them face up to three wastepiles, one to each from left to right. Whenever possible, you may build from the top of any wastepile or from the reserve. A reserve card is only available, however, if at least one of its four sides is free (i.e. not flanked by another card of the reserve).

When stuck, gather the wastepiles from right to left, turn them upside down to form a new stock, shuffle it, fill any gaps in the diamond, and continue play. Three redeals are allowed, in the last of which the cards of the diamond are gathered into the pack and a smaller diamond redealt with only seven cards in the middle row.

Variant: Four redeals are allowed, with a smaller diamond each time. At each redeal shuffle the unused reserve cards into the pack. The second diamond has seven cards in the middle row, the third has five, the fourth three, and the last consists of one card only.

Hill of Difficulty

A nineteenth-century German game, **Der Olymp**, which lives up to its English title.

Take the Aces and Twos and arrange them in two lines making an upside-down 'V', like the sides of a hill.

Deal five cards face up in a row at the bottom of the hill between the two sides, then three more in a row above them, and finally one above the three. These nine make a tableau known as the 'mound'.

The Aces and Twos are bases. Your aim is to build on them in alternating colour and sequence, the Aces up to the Kings (A 3 5 7 9 J K) and the Twos up to the Queens (2 4 6 8 10 Q). 'Alternating colour' means, of course, red Three on black Ace, and so on.

Turn cards from stock one by one, and, if possible, build them on the sides if they fit or else pack them on any card in the bottom row (only) of the mound. Pack in alternating sequence regardless of suit (e.g. any 5 on any 7, etc). If not possible, discard face up to a single wastepile. The top of the wastepile is always available for building or packing where possible.

From the mound, only uppermost cards in the bottom row may be built on the sides. When a space is made in this row, the card immediately above it in the next row (if any) is available, if possible, for building on the sides or packing on the bottom row. After all building and packing have been done, refill gaps in the mound from stock or wastepile. There is no redeal, and the game lives up to its name.

Busy Aces

You could hardly wish for a simpler game than this, though you might find yourself wishing for a redeal.

Deal twelve cards face up in a row. Your aim is to found the Aces, as and when they appear, and build them up in suit and sequence to the Kings. Start, if you can, from the layout, and deal fresh cards to any spaces thereby created.

Turn cards from stock and play them if possible or else discard them face up to a single wastepile. On the twelve cards of the layout, pack downwards in suit, moving only one card at a time. Fill any space with the top card of stock or wastepile.

There is no redeal.

British Constitution

The following elaborate concoction is taken from Lady Cadogan's first patience collection of about 1870, and I often wonder if she invented it. It is not as difficult as it may look from the text, but you are advised not to try it if you are easily upset by Victorian patriotism (or have no sense of humour).

Remove all Aces, Kings and Queens and arrange them in a circle. The Queens are stacked together in the middle, that on top representing 'the Sovereign on her throne'. The Kings, representing bishops and judges, are purely decorative and have no part to play in the proceedings. The Aces represent Parliament, and the object of play is to build all the Aces up in suit to the Jacks.

Next, deal four separate rows of eight cards each, face up. These form 'the constitution', and represent respectively the Privy Council, the Lords, the Commons, and the People.

Turn cards from stock and either play them as described below or else discard them face up to a single wastepile. The top card of the wastepile is always available for entering into the layout, and you might as well know now that there will be no redeal.

The only cards that may be built directly on the Ace piles are uncovered cards in the Privy Council (top row).

Any uncovered card in the bottom three rows may be shifted up into any position in the row immediately above it, where it must either fill a space or else cover a card of opposite colour and next higher in rank, e.g. red Four on black Five, black Three on red Four, etc. Only one card may be moved at a time.

Cards may not be packed on the bottom row. When a gap is made there, it is filled immediately with the top card of the wastepile (preferably) or stock.

Although there is no redeal of the wastepile, the game usually comes out.

Note: You are allowed to leave a gap in the bottom row and continue playing cards directly from stock to wastepile, if you consider this will best advance your game.

British Constitution   An opening layout.

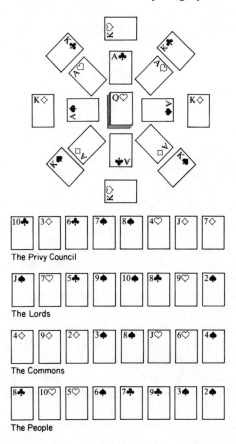

The Privy Council

The Lords

The Commons

The People

Maria

Here are two games of classically simple design to follow the excesses of **British Constitution**, though neither comes out very often.

Deal nine cards face up in a row. Deal nine more across and overlapping them, and continue until you have made four rows. Aim to free the Aces and build them up in suit and sequence to the Kings.

The uncovered card in each column is available for building on a suit sequence if it fits, or packing on another available card. Pack in descending sequence and alternating colour (e.g. black Ten on red Jack, etc.). A space in the layout may be filled with any free card.

Having made as many moves as you can from the layout, turn cards from stock and build or pack them if possible, or else discard them face up to a single wastepile. The top card of the wastepile may always be built or packed if it fits. There is no redeal.

Snake

Deal eight cards face up in a row, then eight more overlapping them, and keep going until you have made eight rows. Your aim is to free the Aces and build them up in suit to the Kings.

The uncovered card at the end of each column is available for building on a suit sequence if it fits, or for packing on another available end-card in descending sequence regardless of suit (e.g. any Ten on any Jack, etc.). A properly packed sequence of any length may be taken as a whole and packed on the end of another column provided that the join follows the rule.

Turn cards from stock and, if possible, build or pack them in accordance with these rules. An unplayable card is added to the bottom of the left-hand column, which takes the place of a wastepile. The last card of this column is always available for building or packing, and may itself be packed on.

There is no redeal, but you may 'worry back' to help the game along (i.e. take the top card of a suit sequence and pack it back on the layout.)

The game is so called because the left-hand column tends to grow very long and may need to be curled round like a snake.

Club

This Victorian game, from the collection of Mary Whitmore-Jones, has a quite attractive layout. Its relation to the title I will leave you to ponder for yourself.

Leave room at the top for a row of eight Aces, your object being to found them as and when they appear and build them up in suit and sequence to the Kings.

Below this empty row, deal eight cards face down in an arc (see

Club The opening layout.

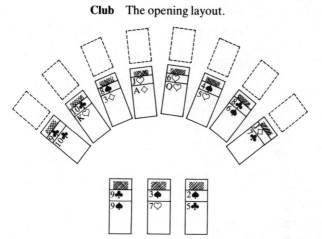

diagram), then two more rows of eight face up across them. This forms the upper half of the layout. Below it, deal a row of three cards face down, then two more rows of three face up across it. This is the lower half.

Turn cards from stock one at a time and play them if possible or else discard them face up to a single wastepile. The turned card or the top of the wastepile may be founded if it is an Ace, built on an Ace-pile if it fits, or packed on an exposed card in the layout. Pack always in descending sequence and alternating colour, moving only one card at a time.

An exposed card in the layout may also be founded, built, or packed on another in accordance with these rules, but with this restriction: no card may be transferred from the lower half of the layout into the upper half, either for packing or for filling a gap, though cards may be moved from the upper to the lower.

There is no redeal and the game does not often come out.

Gargantua (Double Klondike)

We have already met **Klondike** as a very popular one-pack game also known (misleadingly) as **Canfield**. Several versions have been devised for two packs. A good one by Morehead and Mott-Smith is named **Gargantua** after a sixteenth-century giant, the hero of a

Gargantua A game in progress.

stock

wastepile

fantasy by Rabelais, who gives a long list of games that Gargantua enjoyed playing. They include many card games. Not all are identifiable, though it is certain that none of them would have been any form of Patience.

All cards are dealt face down. Deal nine in a row, then a second card on each of the first eight, then a third on each of the first seven, and so on to a ninth on the first pile only. Turn all nine top cards face up. These piles make up the tableau.

Your aim is to found the Aces when possible and build them all up in suit and sequence to the Kings.

Turn cards from stock one at a time and discard them face up to a single wastepile if they cannot be played. The top card of a tableau pile, the top of the wastepile and turned card from stock are all available. An available card may be founded if it is an Ace, or built on an Ace pile if it fits. Or it may be packed on the tableau to form a descending sequence in alternating colour (e.g. red Ten on black Jack, black Nine on red Ten, etc.).

In the tableau, any length of properly packed sequence may be packed as a whole on another top card provided that the join follows the rule. When a face-down card is exposed, turn it face up. A gap in the tableau, made by playing off the last card of a pile, may be filled with any available King, or a packed sequence headed by a King.

The wastepile may be turned and redealt once only. If you redeal twice the game comes out too often to present any challenge.

Batsford

Try this if you do not like games with redeals. Play as in **Gargantua** but deal ten cards to the first row, then nine and so on down to one. If a King becomes available and you have no empty space in the tableau for it, you may lay it to one side in reserve until you can find a proper use for it. A maximum of three Kings may be held in reserve at a time. You may not pack on them, and there is no redeal.

Seven Devils

A two-pack cross between **Demon** and **Klondike** (and **Canfield**, if you count it separately), **Seven Devils** has a wickedly apt title.

All cards are dealt face down. Deal seven in a row, then another row of six overlapping the first six of these, then further rows of five, four, three, two and one. This makes a triangular tableau of seven columns ranging in length from seven cards in the first down to one in the last. Turn the last card of each column face up.

Deal a batch of seven cards face down to one side and turn the top one face up. These form a reserve, and are the 'seven devils' of the title (as you will soon find out).

Your aim is to found the eight Aces as and when they appear, and to build each one up in suit and sequence to its King.

The end card of each column is available for building on an Ace pile if it fits, or for packing on another available card in the tableau. Pack downwards in alternating colour (red 7 on black 8, etc.), moving only one card at a time. Whenever a down-card is cleared, turn it face up. Whenever a column is emptied, refill it with any available card from the tableau or the top card of the stock or wastepile – but not from the reserve.

Turn cards from stock and either build or pack them if possible or else discard them face up to a single wastepile. The top card of the wastepile is always available for building or packing, and should be taken whenever possible as there is no redeal.

The top card of the reserve may only be taken when it can be built on one of the Ace piles. The next below it is then turned face up.

The game does not often succeed, though you may slightly improve your chances (and increase the skill factor) by dealing the 'seven devils' face up and spreading them out so that all are visible. Better the devil you know, as they say . . .

Limited

Limited is so called partly because it limits the amount of packing you can do on the layout, and partly because it offers limited chances of success. However, you can overcome this by redealing the wastepile if you feel that strongly about it.

Deal three rows of cards, face up, with twelve in each row. Do not overlap any cards but keep the rows separate from one another. These form the layout. Your aim is to found the Aces as and when they appear, and build them up in suit and sequence to the Kings.

Turn cards from stock one at a time, discarding any that are unplayable to the top of a single wastepile. The turned card, the top of the wastepile, and the bottom card of each vertical line of three in the layout are available for starting or building on Ace-piles if they fit, or for packing in the layout.

Regard the opening layout as consisting of twelve columns of three cards. Only the lowest card in a column may be moved or packed on, but its removal frees the one above it for use, and the removal of that in turn releases the topmost card. A space made by taking the top card of a column may be filled with any available card from stock, wastepile or bottom of another column.

Only one card may be packed on the bottom card of a column, and that is the card of the same suit and next lower in rank (e.g. ♡6 goes on ♡7, etc.). Two such cards form a couple, which may not be further packed on or moved until both its members can be built on an Ace-pile.

When you run out of stock, turn the wastepile face down and deal the top four cards face up in a row. You may not pack on any of them, but you may use them either for building or, in the layout, for pairing or for filling gaps at the top of emptied columns.

Any of these four that can be taken are then replaced from the new stock, and play continues in this way until you either win or stick. If stuck, you may turn the next card from stock and use it to get the game going again if you can, but if you cannot then the game is lost.

Note: The game does not often come out but does present an intriguing challenge. It is often wise to delay packing or filling gaps until you can make best use of the opportunities they offer.

Colonel

Another patience with a 'limited' rule of packing. It will not often come out – unless, of course, you keep redealing the wastepile, which is against the rules because it never fails.

Deal 36 cards face up in three rows of twelve, without any overlapping. The object is to found the Aces as and when they appear, and build them up in suit and sequence to the Kings.

Throughout play, a card in these rows is 'available' only if there is a gap immediately below it in the next row. All the cards in the bottom row are therefore available, but not until one is taken does the one next above it become available, and so on.

Available cards may be taken for founding if they are Aces, or for building on Ace-piles if they fit, or for packing on one another downwards in suit (e.g. ♣5 on ♣6). However, a card may only be packed on one which is available and lies in the same or a higher row than itself, not on any in a lower row.

Build and pack as far as you can, then turn cards from stock and build or pack them if possible or else discard them face up to a single wastepile. Again, packing takes place only on cards which are available.

The top of the wastepile may be taken for packing or building. A gap made by clearing out a column may be filled with any single available card. Cards may only be moved one at a time. There is no redeal.

Napoleon at St Helena

This early forerunner of **Indian**, (which follows), starts with 40 cards in the tableau and is also known as **Big Forty** or **Forty Thieves**. Lady

Napoleon at St Helena   A game in progress.

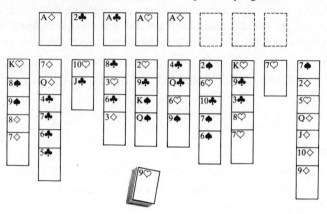

Cadogan called it **Le Cadran** (The Dial), but I think her attention was wandering at the time.

Deal ten cards face up in a row, then three more rows on top of them, overlapping so all are visible. Play to release the Aces and build them up in suit and sequence to the Kings. Turn cards from stock one at a time and build or pack them if possible or else discard them face up to a single wastepile. Pack the tableau downwards in suit (e.g. ♠6 on ♠7, etc.) moving only one card at a time. A space may be filled with any available card. There is no redeal. It rarely comes out.

Indian Patience

Indian does not come out very often, but has a few unusual features which make it worth a try.

Deal ten cards face down in a row. Deal the next ten face up in a row on top of them, and – also face up – another row of ten on top of this. Spread the exposed cards slightly so you can see what they all are. These 30 cards form the tableau.

Your aim is to release the Aces when possible, and build them up in suit and sequence to the Kings.

Turn cards from stock one by one and discard unplayable ones to a single wastepile. Available cards are those exposed in the tableau, the card turned from stock and the top of the wastepile. An available card may be built on an Ace-pile if it fits, or packed on an exposed card in the tableau. Packing takes place in descending sequence and differing suit (e.g. on ♡9 you may pack any Eight except a heart). Only one card may be moved at a time.

When a down-card is exposed, turn it face up. It then becomes a 'protected card', which means you cannot pack on it or move it anywhere except to build it, if possible, on an Ace-pile. Having done so, you fill the space it leaves in the same way as in the original deal – one card face down and two more face up.

There is no redeal, but when the stock is exhausted all 'protected' cards become free for use in the usual way. This helps the game come out more often than it otherwise would.

Hemispheres

This splendid specimen of Victoriana is to be found amongst the pages of the earliest Patience collection published in Britain, that of Lady Cadogan in about 1875. It may look complicated and does take rather a lot of words to describe, but it is really quite simple to play once you get started. **Hemispheres** has a sort of racial theme which may not be found particularly appealing today, but one should not criticise the past for having different values from our own.

As illustrated, take the four black Kings and four red Aces and arrange them in an upright cross with the Kings inside the arms and the Aces outside. These are all base cards. Your aim will be to build on the Aces upwards in suit to the Kings and on the Kings downwards in suit to the Aces.

Next, take two black Aces and two red Kings and place them crossways at the ends of the arms: ♠A at north, ◇K east, ♣A south and ♡K west. These represent 'geographical barriers dividing the races'. They have no part to play in the proceedings and are not touched until the end of the game, when they go on top of the appropriate suit-sequences in a final flourish.

Shuffle the rest of the cards and deal the next twelve face up in a circle around the original cross, so that three lie between each adjacent pair of 'barrier' cards.

Of the six cards in the northern hemisphere (representing European and Asiatic races), only those which are *red* may be used for building and packing. Of those in the south (Africans and Austral-

Hemispheres Opening layout.

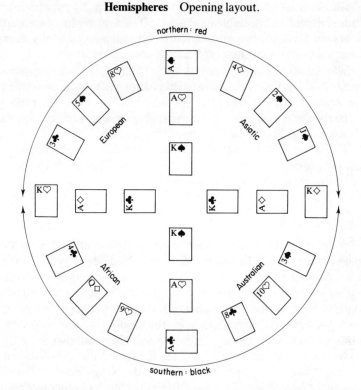

asians), only *black* cards may be used. You may, at any time possible, exchange a black card in the northern hemisphere for a red card in the southern. Start by making any such exchanges you can. Don't worry if there are not the right number of each colour to get them all into their proper hemispheres – you will have other opportunities to swap them over later in the game.

You may now, if possible, take red cards in the northern hemisphere and build them on the bases or pack them on one another *downwards* in suit (e.g. ♡8 on ♡9). Black cards in the southern hemisphere may similarly be built or else packed on one another *upwards* in suit (e.g. ♠9 on ♠8). Any gap in a hemisphere made by taking a card must be filled at once from the top of the stock.

Having gone as far as you can, continue play by turning cards from stock and building them if they fit or packing them on the hemispheres in accordance with the rules above. Put unplayable cards on a single wastepile. The top of the wastepile may be taken for building and packing whenever possible. Lose no opportunity to do so, as there is no redeal.

If you get stuck when no cards remain in stock or waste, you may transfer a card in its 'wrong' hemisphere to a gap, or any, in its right one.

The game should come out more often than not.

Big Ben

Many patience games are based on the design of a clock face. This old one is also known as **Grandfather Clock** and **Father Time**.

Take out the following twelve cards: ♠2-6-10, ♡3-7-J, ♣4-8-Q, ◇5-9-K. Arrange them in a circle, starting with the Six at one o'clock, followed by the Seven at two o'clock, followed by 8, 9, 10, J, Q, K, 2, 3, 4 and finishing with the Five at 12 o'clock.

Deal the next 36 cards face up in twelve batches of three. Lay each batch of three in an overlapping line radiating outwards from a clockface position, the first batch at one o'clock and so on (see diagram).

The twelve inner cards are bases. Your object is to build cards on top of them upwards in suit and sequence (Kings followed by Aces) until each pile is topped by the card whose number corresponds to its clockface position. For example, the ♠6 base at one o'clock is built up to the Ace. A Jack, of course, will represent 11 and a Queen 12 o'clock.

The 36 outer cards form the tableau. The outermost card of each arm of the tableau – the one which overlaps but is not itself overlapped – is available for use. It may be built on an inner clockface position if it fits, or it may be packed on another 'available' card to form a descending suit sequence (e.g. ♡8 on ♡9, ♠K on ♠A, etc.).

Having built and packed as far as you can, turn cards from stock one by one and either build or pack them if possible or else discard them face up to a single wastepile. The top card of the wastepile remains available for building or packing, and should be taken whenever possible as there is no redeal.

Big Ben Opening layout.

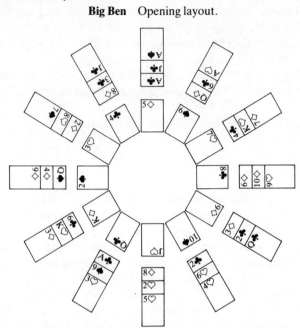

A special rule applies to the twelve arms of the tableau. Whenever one or more arms contains fewer than three cards, you may pause and bring all the short arms back up to three again by dealing fresh cards from the top of the stock (not from anywhere else). You may leave them short until you decide to fill them, but, when you do, you must fill them all and you must do so in clockwise order starting at the earliest clockface position.

Although no redeal of the wastepile is allowed, the game should turn out successfully as often as not.

Quilt

Quilt, also known as **Japanese Rug** and **Indian Carpet**, has a beautiful pattern and is aptly titled from its patchwork appearance. It is also fun to play and comes out more often than not. What more can one ask of a game of patience?

Take an Ace and a King of each suit and set them out as bases at the top or the sides of the table. Your aim is to build the Aces up in

Quilt The opening layout, showing which cards have 'free' short edges to start with.

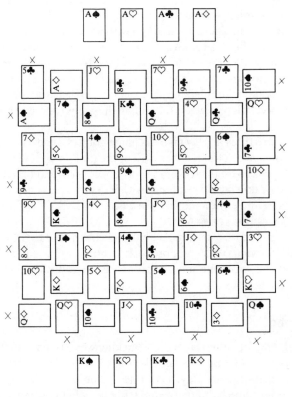

suit and sequence to the Kings and the Kings down in suit and sequence to the Aces.

Shuffle the rest and deal the next sixty-four cards face up in an 8 × 8 square without overlapping and in alternating orientation. That is: lay the first card vertically, the second horizontally, the next vertically, and so on in turn, so that every card in the square has its short sides adjacent to the long sides of its neighbours, and its long sides adjacent to their short ones. (In case of desperation, see diagram.) These form a pattern called the 'quilt'.

Turn cards from stock one by one and build them on Ace or King piles if they fit, or else discard them face up to a single wastepile. The top of the wastepile can always be taken for building if it fits.

Also available for building is any card in the quilt which has at least one of its shorter edges free. To start with, for example, the sixteen cards which appear to be sticking out from the edges of the quilt can be taken. These are marked with an 'x' on the diagram. As soon as one of them is removed, it releases at least one other quilt card for use by freeing one of its short edges. No packing takes place in the quilt, nor are any of its cards replaced when taken. Thus the quilt is gradually nibbled away from the edges and eventually disappears completely when (as usually happens) the game comes out.

Three more rules of play give the game good chances of reaching a happy conclusion. First, a free card of the quilt may, if desired, be taken and packed on the top of the wastepile, provided that it forms an upward or downward sequence with it. The sequence must be of the same suit and either one up or one down in rank, e.g. ♡6 on ♡5 or ♡7, ♣K on ♣Q or ♣A.

Second, a card on top of an Ace pile may be shifted to the top of a King pile – or vice versa – if it properly continues the sequence.

Finally, the wastepile may be turned once and played through again as a new stock.

Backbone

Although the opening layout of **Backbone** is similar to that of **Wheat-Ear** and **Pigtail**, the game belongs to a different family and is more interesting to play. (Another game of similar design is **Herring-Bone**, which differs from **Backbone** only in design details.)

As illustrated, deal 22 cards face up in two separate columns of eleven each, overlapping the cards in each column and laying them angle-wise for pictorial effect. These form the backbone. If any of them are Aces, do not include them in the design but put them to one side as they come out.

Deal the next card face up horizontally at the bottom of the backbone – unless it is a King, in which case bury it in the pack and replace it with the next card.

On either side of the backbone deal four cards face up to represent the 'ribs'.

This completes the layout. Your object is to found all the Aces in a row at the bottom of the design and build them up into thirteen-

Backbone   The opening layout.

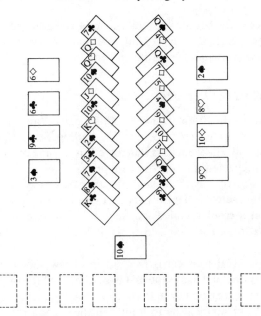

card suit sequences headed by the Kings. Set up any such Aces that may have appeared in the deal. The rest go in position as and when they become available.

Start by playing from the layout as far as possible. The bottom card of the backbone (which I suppose anatomists might refer to as the 'coccyx') is available for building on an Ace-pile if it fits or for packing a card of the 'ribs'. When taken, it releases the two lowest cards of the backbone, and throughout the game the bottom card of each column is always available for packing or building. Packing takes place on the eight 'rib' cards, in suit and descending sequence ($\heartsuit$7 on $\heartsuit$8, etc.), and the exposed card of each rib is available for building on an Ace-pile whenever possible. A gap made by removing the last card of a rib may be filled with any available card, whether from another rib, the backbone, the stock or the wastepile.

Having played as far as you can, turn cards from stock one by one and either build or pack them if possible or else discard them face up to a single wastepile. The top card of the wastepile may be packed or built whenever possible.

Only one redeal of the wastepile is said to be allowed, but, as the chances of success are rather slim, you may prefer to redeal twice and count half a win if you get it out then.

Queen of Italy (Terrace)

I do not know the origin of this delightful game, but it is by far the best of a group which also includes **Falling Star**, **Blondes and Brunettes**, and **The General's Patience**. It is a game of skill and can usually be expected to come out with proper play.

At the top of the table deal eleven cards face up in a row, overlapping them so that only the last one is fully exposed. These cards form a reserve called the 'terrace'. Throughout play, only the card exposed at the end is available for entering into the game.

Below it, deal four cards face up in a row, not overlapping. Choose any one of these as the first base-card, and transfer the other three to the start of yet a third row, also not overlapping one another. Your aim will be to found, in the second row, the other seven cards of the same rank as the first base – as and when they become available – and to build them up into thirteen-card suit sequences, turning the corner from King to Ace as necessary.

You should note at this point that considerable importance attaches to the rank you choose as first base. It must be one which enables you to work cards off the terrace as early as possible. For example, if the card at the buried end of the terrace is a King, it would be fatal to choose a King as first base, and hardly wiser to choose a Queen or Jack, as one of the main sequences could not then be started much before the end of play. An Ace base, however, would be ideal.

Having made your wisest possible choice, complete the third row by dealing as many more cards as necessary to bring it up to nine cards long. These nine start the tableau. Exposed cards from the tableau may be built on the main sequences upwards in suit, or packed on one another downwards in sequence and alternating colour (e.g. black Ace on red Two, red King on black Ace, etc.). Only one card may be moved at a time. The available card of the

Queen of Italy Of the first four cards dealt after the reserve, ◇ has been selected as the most promising base and the other three repositioned at the start of the row beneath it. This row has then to be completed with further cards dealt as they come.

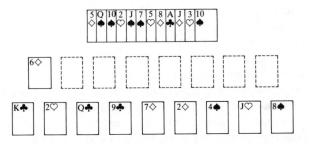

terrace may only be built on a main sequence, not packed on the tableau.

Having played as far as you can, turn cards from stock and either build or pack them if possible or else discard them face up to a single wastepile. The top card of the wastepile at any given time is available for packing or building if it fits, and should be taken if at all possible as there is no redeal.

A gap made in the tableau may be filled with any available card from the tableau, or from the top of the stock or wastepile.

Grace: If you run out of stock and then find yourself unable to bring the game out, you may allow yourself to borrow a grace permitted by a similar game called 'General's'. Under its rules, you may turn the wastepile once and start going through it as a new stock. But you may only continue for as long as you can enter the cards into the game: you may not discard any to a wastepile the second time round.

Staircase (Step-Up)

A distant relative of the preceding **Queen of Italy**, **Staircase** is also a game of skill and should succeed nearly as often as you play it well. (I don't like changing the titles of established games if I can help it, for fear of causing confusion, but **Step-up** is an awkward title and the change to **Staircase** enables a few other terminological improvements to be made.)

Deal thirteen cards face up in a row, not overlapping. These form a reserve called the 'landing'. Deal the next card face up to start another row above the landing. This card is the first base. Your aim will be to complete the top row with the other seven cards of the same rank as the first base as and when they become available, and to build them all up into thirteen-card suit sequences, turning the corner from King to Ace as necessary.

Below the landing, deal nine cards face up in a row (not overlapping) to start a tableau known as the 'staircase'.

Throughout play, cards may only be built onto main sequences from the landing: they cannot come direct from the staircase. Those that are taken for building will leave gaps, of course, and staircase cards may then be used for filling the gaps in the landing.

Start by playing from the landing any possible base cards and any that can be built on a main sequence. Refill gaps in the landing from the staircase, and in the staircase from the stock.

Cards in the staircase may be packed on one another downwards in alternating colour (red Ace on black Two, black King on red Ace, etc.), only one being moved at a time, and gaps filled from stock.

When you can go no further, turn cards from stock one by one and either pack them in the staircase, if possible, or else discard them face up to a single wastepile. The top card of the wastepile can always be taken for packing, and should be taken whenever possible as there is no redeal.

Remember that no card may be built on a main sequence except from the landing, and no card played to the landing except from the staircase. A gap in the landing need not be filled immediately, but can be held open for up to three more turns from the stock, after which it *must* be filled with an exposed card from the staircase.

British Square

The patriotic title may well suggest a Victorian origin, and, sure enough, this one is to be found in Lady Cadogan's second Patience book. She, however, took it from an earlier German anthology and retained its original title, **Das Quadrat**, i.e. simply 'Square'. I have not discovered who Briticised it.

Your aim is to found four Aces of different suits as and when they appear, and on each one to build a 26-card suit sequence. Each sequence is to run from Ace up to King, to be followed then by the second King and all the other duplicate cards of its suit back down to the Ace.

Deal sixteen cards face up in a 4 × 4 square without overlapping. Take out any Aces that can be used as base cards and put them to one side, and add any other cards from the square which can legally be built upon them. Fill any vacancies in the square from the stock, and keep going as far as you can. You may also pack cards in the square on top of one another in suit and either ascending or descending sequence (e.g. ◇8 on ◇9 or ◇7). Whichever direction you choose to pack in, however, must be adhered to – you may not change direction in the same pile; nor may any card be packed on a King or an Ace. Only one card may be moved at a time, but this is no great restriction, as you can always play cards off singly from an ascending pile to a descending pile and vice versa.

A gap made in the square must be filled at once from the top of the stock (or wastepile, when there is one). It may not be filled with a card taken from elsewhere in the square.

Having got as far as you can from the opening position, turn cards from stock one by one and either build or pack them if possible or else discard them face up to a single wastepile. The top card of the wastepile remains available for building and packing, and should be taken whenever possible as there is no redeal.

Interregnum

This is a good game. It has a simple layout requiring no illustration, gives plenty of scope for skill, and can usually be expected to come out with proper play.

Deal – face up and without overlapping – two rows of eight cards, with room for a third row between them. Cards in the top row are called 'indicators'. Those in the bottom row are the first cards of eight wastepiles.

Your aim is to found eight base cards in the empty middle row, and build them up into thirteen-card sequences, regardless of suit and turning the corner from King to Ace as necessary. The base card for each position is to be one rank higher than the indicator card immediately above it. For example, if the first indicator is a Jack, the base beneath it will be a Queen, to be followed by King,

Ace, Two, etc. up to Ten and finally crowned with the Jack indicator.

Start by founding or building any cards possible from the bottom row, but do not replace them. Then deal eight more cards across the bottom row, pause, and do any more building that may be possible. Continue in this way, dealing eight more across the bottom row every time you can do no further building.

Overlapping cards in the bottom row may be spread towards you so that all are visible, but only the exposed card of each pile may be taken for building. Its removal, of course, releases the one beneath it for the same purpose.

A gap in the bottom row is not to be filled except as a result of dealing the next row of eight. When dealing a new row, all eight must be dealt before you may start building again.

When you run out of stock, you ought to be able to complete the sequences by playing off cards from the bottom row. If not, the game is lost.

Mathematical

The following game, also known as **Senior Wrangler**, is both complicated and maddening. But as it usually comes out all right with careful play there is not really much to complain about.

Take out eight cards from Ace to Eight inclusive and lay them in a row at the top. Leave room for a second row beneath them, and beneath the empty second row deal the remainder out, face down, in eight piles of twelve cards each. Finally, turn these piles face up.

Your aim is to found eight base cards in the empty row, as and when they become available, and to build them up into thirteen-card numerical sequences regardless of suit. For this purpose Jacks count as 11, Queens 12 and Kings 13, and Kings are consecutive with Aces. The sequences are built up in leaps as indicated by base card – see table opposite.

Now we come to the tricky bit. Each base card is to be twice the value of the card in the row above it, so they will be, in order: 2, 4, 6, 8, 10, Q, A, 3. Queen is 12, which is twice the Six above it. Ace counts as 14, and Three as 16 – and if you can't see why, then you shouldn't be playing such a silly game in the first place!

Cards for building may come from the piles in the bottom row or (if it helps) from other main sequences. Only the current top card of a pile can be taken, of course.

When stuck, take up the first pile in the bottom row and deal cards from it one at a time across the row, the first card going to the space it leaves and the rest to the tops of the next piles. You may look through the pile you are about to deal and decide whether to hold it face down or up when dealing. In other words, you can deal it out from whichever end you prefer.

Play again until stuck, then take the second pile and deal it out in the same way. Continue until the game either comes out or blocks after you have redealt the eighth pile, in which case you've had it.

Just for reference, the sequences go as follows:

A	2	3	4	5	6	7	8	9	10	J	Q	K
2	4	6	8	10	Q	A	3	5	7	9	J	K
3	6	9	Q	2	5	8	J	A	4	7	10	K
4	8	Q	3	7	J	2	6	10	A	5	9	K
5	10	2	7	Q	4	9	A	6	J	3	8	K
6	Q	5	J	4	10	3	9	2	8	A	7	K
7	A	8	2	9	3	10	4	J	5	Q	6	K
8	3	J	6	A	9	4	Q	7	2	10	5	K

Babette

This game has some unusual features, which are continued in its more complicated relative **Triumph**.

Deal eight cards face up in a row near the top of the table. Leave room above them for a row of base cards which you will found as and when they become available. The bases are to be an Ace and a King of each suit. You will then aim to build the Aces up in suit and sequence to the Kings, and the Kings down in suit and sequence to the Aces.

Do any founding and building that may be possible from the first row, but leave the gaps unfilled.

When stuck, deal another row of eight beneath the first, without overlapping them. Throughout the game keep dealing a new row of eight beneath the previous one whenever you can get no further. This will extend the layout into eight columns, each of which will consist partly of cards and partly of spaces. From the layout you may take for building any card whose bottom edge lies immediately above a space, but not one which lies immediately above a card.

You may also, if it helps (and fits), transfer a card from the top of one sequence to that of another going in the opposite direction.

If the game fails when you run out of cards, you may redeal in the following way. Squeeze each column into a pile of cards, with the lowest of the column at the top of the pile. Make a new stock by adding the piles together in the same direction as the deal, turn it upside down and start playing again.

The original rules allow only one such redeal, but as the game rarely comes out you may want to count half a win for doing it in two.

Stag Party

The male chauvinist version of **Babette** stands more chance of reaching a successful conclusion, as you might expect. Play as described above, but with these differences.

Found all eight Sixes and all eight Fives as they become available. Build the Sixes up in suit to the Jacks and the Fives down in suit to the Kings.

Each time you deal a row of eight, pause before playing to discard any Queens from it, thus creating helpful spaces. There is – surely? – no redeal.

Triumph

Triumph is a more complicated relative of **Babette**. It is similar to, but more challenging than, a game called **Four Intruders**, and almost identical with another known as **Senate** or **Congress**.

Set the Aces up in a row at the top of the table. Your aim is to build them up in suit and sequence to the Kings.

Deal a row of eight cards beneath them, and another four in a column to one side – all face up and none overlapping.

Build any cards that may be possible from the first row, fill the spaces they leave from stock, and keep building and filling until you can go no further.

You may also build and replace any cards that may be possible from the column. Furthermore, column cards may be packed on one another in suit and descending sequence, and any length of properly packed sequence may be transferred to another column card provided that the the join follows the rule. For the time being, however, the column and the row(s) are separate: no card may be transferred from one to the other.

When stuck, deal another row of eight beneath the first, without overlapping. Play off any cards that can be built. The removal of a card releases the one immediately above it for building if it fits.

Every time you get stuck, refill from stock all the gaps in the rows, following the same order from the top downwards. Do any building that may be possible and fill the gaps again. When you have filled gaps and can do no more building, deal a new row of eight beneath the last. Then pause and play again in the same way. A card may only be taken from the rows if its bottom edge is free, i.e. if there is no card beneath it.

If the game blocks when you have run out of stock, the following 'grace' is permitted. You may remove any four cards from the rows and either build them on main sequences or pack them on piles in the column – though you may not play more than one such card to the *same* column. You may also build or pack any card lying immediately above a space so created (but not any further cards lying above that).

If you succeed in using at least four cards in this way, you may repeat the grace by drawing another four cards.

The grace may not be taken more than twice, but the game will usually have come out by then anyway.

Virginia Reel

Another invention of Morehead and Mott-Smith, **Virginia Reel** is probably the best member of a family represented in older books under the title **Royal Parade**, and is also known as **Hussars** or **Royal Procession**. It looks unnecessarily complicated at first reading, but is quite easy to play once you get down to it, and rather fun even if it does not come out very often.

We should start by noting that all the Twos, Threes and Fours will be base cards, and that they are to be built up in suit by intervals of three, like this:

$$2 \quad 5 \quad 8 \quad J$$
$$3 \quad 6 \quad 9 \quad Q$$
$$4 \quad 7 \quad 10 \quad K$$

Although the Aces do not fit into this scheme, they will be found to have one small but useful role to play.

Start by founding a Two, a Three and a Four, of different suits, down the top left of the table. To the right of each deal seven more cards in a row, face up and non-overlapping. You will be wanting to get all the Twos into the top row, the Threes into the middle and the Fours into the bottom of these three rows as the opportunity arises, because base cards cannot start being built on until they are in their proper rows.

Remove any Aces from the opening deal and discard them. You may now transfer any base cards that may be lying in their wrong row to their right row, either by playing them to gaps left by the removal of Aces, or by exchanging them for one another on a one-to-one basis.

Next, deal eight more cards in a new row lower down to start the reserve. Whenever the game blocks, deal eight more across them and continue as before. When an Ace turns up, throw it away and deal the next card in its place.

The rules of building are as follows. A base card may only be built on if it is in the proper row, as explained above. It must be built in

Virginia Reel　Opening layout.

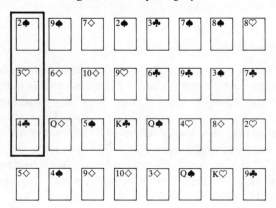

suit and in intervals of three. The building card may come from the top of a pile in the reserve or from anywhere in the top three rows. However, a card may not be taken from these rows unless the gap it leaves can be filled immediately with a Two, Three or Four taken from the reserve. This is the only way in which base cards can be entered into the game. And, of course, if they are entered into the 'wrong' row, they cannot be built upon until they can be exchanged for other base cards also in their wrong rows.

There is no redeal, but one grace is permissible. If the game blocks when you have run out of cards, you may try to get it going again by removing any one card buried in the reserve piles and building it on the appropriate main sequence.

Salic Law

An old game, if not quite so old as the title suggests, **Salic Law** is full of variety and should come out as often as not. (The 'law' referred to is an early medieval one designed to prevent royal succession passing through the female line.) The variation called **Spenser's 'Faerie Queen'** – a title for which I accept no responsibility whatever – should be even more successful.

Leave space at the top of the table for two rows of cards and start a third row with a King drawn from the pack. Start dealing cards face up on the King, overlapping one another so that they grow into a column towards you. As the Aces come out, put them in a row above the King. Queens, likewise, are dealt to a row above the Aces.

Whenever a King appears, start a new column, with the King at the top next to the previous one. The opening layout, when complete, will consist of a row of Queens, a row of Aces and a row of Kings, the Kings all heading columns of various lengths.

Your aim is to build the Aces up into eleven-card sequences headed by Jacks, regardless of suit.

To play, simply take cards from the exposed ends of the columns and build them on the Ace-piles one by one. You may not transfer a card from one column to another. However, when a King becomes uncovered, you may temporarily move one card onto it from the end of another column to keep the game going.

Salic Law   The opening layout also applies – apart from the Queen and Ace rows – to **Faerie Queen**, **Picture Gallery** and **Royal Patience**.

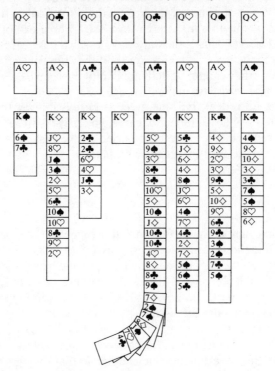

Spenser's 'Faerie Queen'

The previous game comes from Lady Cadogan's first series of patience games with its title given in French. This variant, appearing in her second series, is presumably intended to be more patriotic.

Deal as if for **Salic Law**, but leave the Queens where they fall instead of making them into a separate row. Your aim is then to build the Aces up in suit and sequence to the Queens.

Cards exposed at the ends of columns may be taken for building or packed on one another in descending sequence regardless of suit (e.g. any Jack on any Queen). Only one card may be moved at a time. Any available card may be packed on an exposed King, and may itself be packed on in the usual way.

Picture Gallery

This relative of **Salic Law** is also known as **Intrigue**.

Leaving room for two rows at the top, play a King to the start of a third row, and deal cards face up on the King – spreading into a column – until you reach an Ace or another King. Kings go in a row next to the first one and Aces into a row above the Kings. Each King heads a new column of cards.

Aim to build the Aces upwards in sequence and alternating colour (e.g. red A, black 2, red 3, etc.). As Queens become available, found them in a row above the Aces and build them downwards in sequence and alternating colour. Any card on top of a Queen-down sequence may be transferred to the top of an Ace-up sequence when it fits. Your eventual aim is, in fact, to clear all cards off the Queens, thus finishing with a middle row of Jacks sand-wiched between a row of Queens and a row of Kings (as in **Salic Law**).

Exposed cards on the columns may be packed on one another in alternating colour and either ascending or descending sequence. For example, on a red Five you may play a black Four or a black Six. Only one card may be moved at a time, but you may play up or down ad lib in the same column – you need not keep packing in the same direction.

In the normal course of events you may not play any card to an exposed King. You are, however, allowed two 'graces' during the game. On one occasion only, you may play any available black card to a red King, and on another you may play any available red card to a black King. In both cases you may continue packing on the card so moved.

Royal Patience

As above, start with a King and deal cards into columns headed by the Kings as they turn up. Leave Aces and Queens where they fall. Your aim is to found a row of Aces above the Kings (as and when they become available) and to build them up in suit and sequence to the Queens.

Available cards may be packed on one another downwards in alternating colour. Only one card may be moved at a time, and an exposed King may be packed only with a Queen of opposite colour.

Individual exposed cards may also be taken and held to one side in reserve, though no more than eight at a time. Reserve cards may then be taken for building or packing back on the columns as the occasion demands.

Lady of the Manor

. . . or **La Châtelaine**, to give her her French title, comes from an even older book than Lady Cadogan's. It has a pleasing design and is quite interesting to play, but allows little opportunity for the exercise of skill and does not often turn out successfully. If you like the general idea you may care to try my revision of it under the title **Archway** on the following page.

Arrange the eight Aces in two rows of four near the bottom of the board. Immediately below them deal four piles of cards face down, with twelve in each pile. Then turn each pile face up so that you can see the top card.

Deal the remaining cards into twelve piles arching over the bottom rows, sorting all the Twos into the first pile, Threes into the second, and so on, with Kings in the twelfth. There will be differing numbers of cards in these piles, from nought to eight.

Your aim is to build the Aces upwards into thirteen-card sequences regardless of suit. For this purpose you take and build a top

Lady of the Manor   Opening layout.

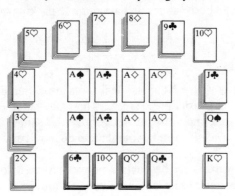

card from the four central piles whenever possible – which is not very often – or else take what you need from the twelve piles sorted into order. (All these cards are available, not just the ones on top.)

There is no redeal.

Variation: In **My Lady's Patience** the two packs are kept separate. The four central piles then contain 48 different cards of one pack and the arch twelve piles of four cards each. This version is slightly easier.

Archway

I devised **Archway** as an extension of **Lady of the Manor** offering more scope for skill and rather more chances of success, though it still comes out less than half the time. The layout, you will observe, now even has a portcullis.

Archway   Opening layout.

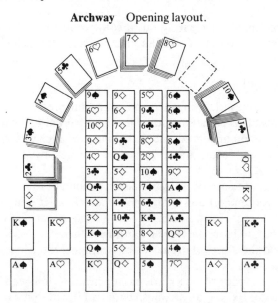

Take out an Ace and a King of each suit. Arrange them in two squares of four cards each, with one square on either side at the bottom of the board, and enough room between the two squares for a row of four cards. These are all bases. Your aim is to build the

Aces up in suit to the Kings and the Kings down in suit to the Aces.

Deal four cards face up in a row near the top of the board, and keep dealing more rows of four across them – spreading the cards downwards towards you into columns – until you have made twelve rows and used up 48 cards.

Deal the remaining cards face up into thirteen piles forming a semicircular arch around the columns. Each pile is reserved to one rank. That is, the first pile is for Aces, the second for Twos, and so on, the thirteenth being for Kings. There will be varying numbers of cards in these piles – some may not have any at all.

The exposed card at the near end of each column is available for building on an Ace or King pile if it fits. Also available for building are *all* the cards in the arch, not just the ones lying on top.

During play, the top card of an Ace sequence may be reversed onto the top of the same-suit King sequence if it fits, and vice versa, though Aces and Kings may not themselves be transferred in this way.

A space made by clearing out a column may be filled with an available card from the end of another column if this helps.

Tournament

Amongst games claiming a Napoleonic flavour is to be found **Napoleon's Flank**, otherwise known as **La Nivernaise**. An improvement on it soon appeared under the name **Maréchal Saxe**, which Morehead and Mott-Smith improved further by renaming it **Tournament**.

Starting at the top of the table deal a column of four cards (face up, not overlapping) down the left side and another four down the right. These eight form a reserve. Leave enough space between the two columns to found an Ace and a King of each suit. Your aim will be to build the Aces up in suit to the Kings and the Kings down in suit to the Aces.

Below this space deal six cards face up in a row, followed by three more rows of six so that you finish with six piles of four cards each, which form the tableau. (It helps to spread them slightly so that all cards in a pile are identifiable.) At any moment in the game the 'available' cards are all those in the reserve plus all the topmost cards in the tableau. Start by founding any Aces and Kings that may be available and replacing them from stock. You will need at least one of each to get the game going, and may therefore draw them from stock if necessary.

Play by taking any available cards that are suitable and building them on the base cards. A space made by taking a card from the reserve may be filled with any exposed card from the tableau, but not from the stock. It need not be filled immediately, but may be held open until a convenient card becomes available on the tableau. A space made by clearing out a pile of cards in the tableau may be filled from stock by dealing four more cards into it.

When stuck, deal 24 more cards to the tableau, four to each pile in turn, and continue play. If there are not enough to go round on the last deal, just take it as far as you can.

If the game blocks when you have run out of cards, redeal by adding together all the piles in the same order in which you dealt them. Then, holding the new stock face up, deal them out again in rows of six until they are all out, and continue play.

Two such redeals are allowed, making three deals in all. One 'grace' may be taken during the course of each of these deals – namely, you may transfer the top card of an Ace-pile to that of a King-pile (or vice versa) if it properly continues the sequence and proves helpful to do so.

Spider

In most patience games you build up sequences in one part of the layout – on the 'bases' or 'foundations' – and may pack cards in the opposite direction in another – the 'tableau'. **Spider** is the chief member of an unusual family in which building and packing are combined in the same layout. (You may already have tried the one-pack relatives **Will o' the Wisp**, **Scorpion** and **Curds and Whey**, described earlier.) Others follow in the next few pages. They do not come out very often, but are quite challenging to play.

Deal six piles of four cards each, face down. Put these piles at the top of the board in a row, and next to them deal another four piles with five cards in each one – also face down. Then turn the top cards face up. These piles start the 'tableau'. Your aim is to expose Kings in the tableau when you can, and then pack them in suit and descending sequence to the Aces. Completed sequences must be discarded from the tableau before the game is won, but they need not all be discarded at the same time and you do not have to discard each one the moment you finish it.

Now see how far you can get with the play before dealing any more cards. Exposed cards may be packed on one another in descending sequence regardless of suit, and these may be spread towards you in columns so all are visible. You may pack the whole or part of any such sequence onto an exposed card if it fits. When a down-card is exposed, turn it face up. Should you empty a pile, you may fill the gap with any exposed card or suit sequence. Kings may not be packed on Aces, but may be moved into gaps.

When stuck, or earlier if you prefer, first fill any gaps with exposed cards, then deal ten more cards across the ends of the columns, and finally continue play. When you complete a full sequence running from King to Ace in the same suit, remove it from the tableau at any convenient time.

There is no redeal. With skilful play you can hope to win about half the time. You may count half a win for getting six suit sequences out. (If seven come out, of course, so will the eighth.)

Microbe

For this Victorian game you start with the two packs separated from each other, not both shuffled together.

From the first, deal eleven cards face down in a row, then eleven face up and overlapping them, then eleven more down and eleven up again. Shuffle the last eight cards into the other pack.

Your aim is to complete eight thirteen-card sequences ('microbes') in this layout, running from King down to Ace in *alternating* colour, and to discard them from the layout as and when convenient.

Exposed cards at the ends of columns are packed on one another in descending sequence and alternating colour, down-cards being turned face up as they become exposed. A properly packed sequence may be packed as a whole on another suitable card. A space made by clearing out a column may be filled with any exposed card or sequence.

Whenever necessary, or useful, deal another card to the end of each column and continue play. After running out of stock you may no longer fill gaps made by clearing out the columns.

Mrs Mop

This spidery game was devised by Charles Jewell and is definitely one of skill. You will find it appropriately named, even if you do not know whom after.

Deal all the cards face up in rows of thirteen, overlapping the eight rows to save space. Regard this tableau as thirteen columns of eight. As in **Spider**, your aim is to make eight thirteen-card suit sequences running from King to Ace within the tableau.

Cards at the exposed ends of the columns are to be packed on one another in descending sequence regardless of suit, though Kings may not be packed on Aces. Exposed cards must be moved one at a time, unless they lie at the end of a properly packed sequence of two or more cards in the same suit, in which case the sequence must be moved as a whole. (It need not, however, be packed onto a card of the same suit.)

A gap made by clearing out a column may be filled with any exposed card or suit sequence. Completed thirteen-card suit sequences from King to Ace are removed from the tableau.

Success depends largely on mopping up individual columns so as to leave spaces for the transference of awkward cards or part-sequences.

Rouge et Noir

One of several different games sharing the same title (unfortunately), this is a cunning and ingenious composition by Charles Jewell. It is not a full-blooded spider, as only half the sequences are formed within the tableau.

Make a 45-card triangle by dealing nine cards in a row face down, then eight across and overlapping them, followed by seven, six and so on down to one. Turn the end cards face up. Regard this triangle as consisting not of nine columns but of ten, with (as yet) no cards in the last 'column'.

Your aim is to make eight thirteen-card sequences, four of them running from King down to Ace within the triangle, and four from

Ace up to King outside the triangle, Aces being taken and founded as they become available. The downward sequences must be headed by two red Kings and two black ones, and run in *alternating colour* (red on black, black on red, etc.). The upward sequences must be founded on two red Aces and two black ones, and run in *similar colour* (red on red, black on black, but otherwise regardless of suit).

Exposed cards in the triangle may be packed on one another in descending sequence and alternating colour. Any length of properly packed sequence may be taken as a whole and packed on a suitable exposed card, and a complete thirteen-card sequence from King to Ace is to be removed entirely from the triangle – though not until you wish it.

A down-card is turned face up when exposed. A gap made by clearing out a column may be filled only with a King or a properly packed sequence headed by a King. Remember that such a gap already exists because of the initially empty 'tenth column'.

Play as far as you can or will, then pause and deal ten more cards, one to the foot of each column or gap as the case may be. There will, of course, be only nine cards on the last deal.

Note: The game seems so difficult that I wonder whether I have misunderstood George Hervey's description of it (in a former version of *Card Games for One*). He does not explicitly state that Kings may not be built on Aces, yet his description of an illustrative position can be taken to imply such a restriction.

It may also be permissible to pack a card back from an Ace pile into the triangle.

King Edward

I dare say the title dates this rather regal spider, which comes from one of Mary Whitmore Jones's later collections. It is a nice game, but rather hard to crown with success.

The aim is to finish up with eight thirteen-card suit sequences, each running from King down to Ace in alternating colour.

Deal eight cards face up in a row, then pause and do any packing that may be possible – downwards, in alternating colour, and moving only one card at a time. You may take out any Aces and put them to one side for the time being, and Twos as well unless there are Threes to pack them on. But you may never hold out two *identical* cards other than Aces. Do not fill any gaps.

When ready, deal another row of eight cards across, overlapping previous cards or filling gaps as the case may be. Play again, packing where possible and holding out Aces and unpackable Twos.

Repeat the process of dealing and packing until you run out of cards. This completes the first half of the game.

In the second half the rules of play are more helpful. Cards available for packing are those at *either* end of each column, and packing is not restricted to individual cards but may be carried out with any length of properly packed sequence starting from either end of a column.

A gap made by clearing out a column may be filled with any available card or packed sequence. A complete King-Ace sequence is not discarded from the layout, though it may (presumably) be shifted into an empty column. Any Aces and Twos held out during the deal may be packed into the layout whenever they fit.

Note: This game is quite hard to bring out, and I may have misinterpreted some of Whitmore Jones's rules. (She was always the dearest but never the clearest of writers.) It may well be permissible to fill vacancies and pack entire sequences in the first half of the game, that is, before all the cards have been dealt out. She is, however, explicit on the fact that Kings are not to be packed on Aces.

German Patience

Another member of the spider family (*arachnidae*), **German Patience** is quite exasperating. You often think it is going to come out all right, but it invariably manages to let you down. It has long been one of my favourite games, even though I have never won it. I think it must be pretty old, but have not been able to track it down to source.

Deal eight cards face up in a row. Your eventual aim is to turn this row into eight piles of thirteen cards, each in ascending sequence regardless of suit. Whatever the bottom card is of any given pile, the top card will be one rank lower. For example, a sequence based on a

Jack will finish up with a Ten. (Kings are followed by Aces, of course.)

Start – if possible – by packing available cards on one another in ascending sequence regardless of suit (e.g. any Two on any Ace, etc.). Fill the gaps immediately from stock, so that there are always eight bases in position.

Having got as far as you can, start turning cards from stock one by one. Play them to the tops of piles if they continue the sequence, or else discard them face up to a single wastepile.

Throughout the game you may transfer any top card to the top of another pile if it fits. You should especially try to work cards off the wastepile in this way, as there is no redeal. This can be helped by clearing spaces amongst the piles whenever you can.

It is important to keep track of the base card of each pile, so that you will know when to stop building it. Do this by making each one stick out from the bottom of the pile. When you complete the sequence, turn the top card face down to show it has been closed.

Although there is no redeal, you may, when the stock is exhausted, extract and play the card at the buried end of the wastepile. But this is only allowed once – grudgingly, at that – and is rarely helpful in any case.

Note: As described, this game is virtually impossible to get out – even if you assume (though there is no justification for it) that a completed pile may be removed from the board leaving a new space to be filled. I suggest you allow at least one redeal, and count yourself lucky if you get it out even then.

Higgledy-Piggledy

A wonderfully uninhibited game for untidy people.

Shuffle two packs together and throw them all over the table. Try to ensure that they all land face down. Turn down those which don't, mix them up a bit and clear a space in the middle. Take any card and lay it face up in this space as the first base. Your aim is to build it up into a thirteen-card suit sequence, turning the corner from King to Ace as necessary. The other seven cards of the same rank, as and when they appear, must also be made into bases and built into thirteen-card sequences.

Higgledy-Piggledy A typical game in progress.

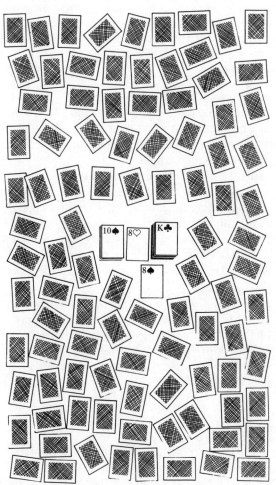

Pick up down-cards at random and either use them for building sequences or else discard them face up to any of four wastepiles. The top card of any wastepile may be taken for building whenever it fits.

When none are left face down, play as far as you can from the top of the wastepiles. When stuck, take one of the four wastepiles and deal it out in rotation to the other three. When stuck again, deal another onto the other two, then either of these onto the other. If you do not get it out when only one wastepile is left you have lost the game.

Above and Below

A much neater game than **Higgledy-Piggledy**. What isn't?

Separate the two packs, shuffle each, and place both together. Deal a card face up to start a row in the middle. This is the first 'indicator'. As others of the same rank become available add them to the row until all eight are out.

Four cards of different suits and one rank *higher* than the indicators (e.g. Jacks if the indicators are Tens, etc.) are to be founded as bases *above* the indicators, when they appear, and built into *ascending* thirteen-card suit sequences. Four of different suits one rank *lower* (e.g. Nines in the above example) are similarly to be founded in a row below it to be built into *descending* thirteen-card suit sequences. Use an indicator, of course, as the thirteenth card for a finished sequence.

Turn cards from stock and play them if possible or else discard them to any of four wastepiles. Cards for building may come from the top of these piles or be reversed from the top of one main sequence to the other of the same suit. Having run out of cards, gather up the four wastepiles into a single stock and play through it again, this time discarding to only one wastepile. There is no further redeal.

Squaring the Circle

This game is closely related to the immediately preceding ones, though its geometry might appear to put it in a class of its own at first sight. The title refers to an unsolvable mathematical problem invented by the ancient Greeks – namely, how to construct a square exactly equal in area to a given circle. It is the sort of problem which, like that of generating perpetual motion, has only ever been solved by cranks.

Take an Ace of each suit and arrange them in a square at the centre of the board. These are bases. Deal the next twelve cards around them in a circle. These form a reserve.

Squaring the Circle Opening layout.

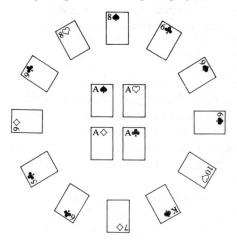

Your aim is to build four 26-card piles based on the Aces. The sequence in each pile must follow suit and is to consist of two interlocking sequences which alternately ascend and descend. In other words, it goes:

A K 2 Q 3 J 4 10 5 9 6 8 7 7 8 6 9 5 10 4 J 3 Q 2 K A

This is the only complication, the rest of the game being fairly conventional.

Start by building from the reserve any Kings and other cards that will continue sequences, and refill the gaps from stock.

When stuck, turn cards from stock one by one and either build them if possible or else discard them face up to any of four wastepiles. At any time during play you may build a card onto a sequence from the top of a wastepile or from the reserve. A gap in the reserve must be filled from the top of a wastepile, or from stock if none are left going to waste.

If the game has not been won by the time you run out of stock, gather up the piles onto a new stock (without shuffling) and play through it a second time in the same way as before.

A second redeal is not permitted, and in any case should not often be necessary.

Double Pyramid

Deal 21 cards face up in the shape of a pyramid, or upside-down 'V', with one at the top and ten down each slide. (I meant to type 'side', but I think 'slide' is more descriptive!) These act as a reserve.

Deal the next card face up inside and at the top of the pyramid. This is the first base. The other seven cards of the same rank will also act as bases, and are to be founded, as and when they appear, inside the pyramid in a row of three followed by a row of four. Your aim is to build these up into thirteen-card suit sequences, turning the corner from King to Ace as necessary.

Turn cards from stock and either build them if possible or else

Double Pyramid   Opening layout.

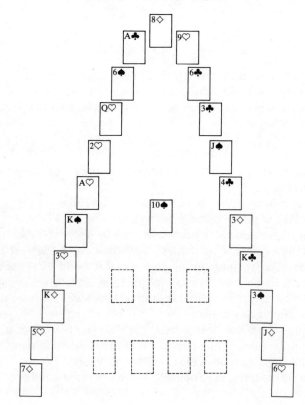

discard them face up to any of four wastepiles forming a base to the pyramid. The top card of a wastepile may be taken for building at any time. So may a card from the reserve, but it is not replaced.

There is no redeal, but the game usually comes out.

Flip-Flop

I have forgotten the source of this natty little game. All I can remember is that I exchanged its original title (**Eight Aces**) for something more distinctive.

Take out all eight Aces and put them in a row as bases. Your object is build each one up into a thirteen-card suit sequence headed by the King.

Turn cards from stock and either build them if possible or else discard them face up to any of six wastepiles. The top card of a wastepile may be taken for building whenever possible.

When all cards have been dealt and no further play is possible, take the top card of each wastepile, replace it face *down* at the bottom of its pile (this action is the 'flip') and continue play. Do the same when stuck again, and so on.

When a down-card eventually comes to the top again, turn it face up ('flop') and continue play. No more flip-flopping may be carried out and there is no redeal.

The game should succeed more often than not.

Grandfather

Grandfather's Patience, to give it its full title, is said to be one of the oldest known. It is a two-pack version of **Sir Tommy** (see page 27).

Deal twenty cards face up in two rows of ten. These form a reserve called the 'promenade'. Your aim is to found an Ace and a King of each suit (as and when they appear) and to build the Aces up in suit to the Kings and the Kings down in suit to the Aces.

Take out any Aces and Kings from the promenade to use as foundations, and build any cards on them that will fit. Fill up the gaps and do the same again. Repeat until you can play no further.

Continue play by turning cards from stock one by one. If a turned card can be built, build it. If not, either discard it face up to a single wastepile, or else use it to cover any single card in the promenade.

Note that no position in the promenade may contain more than two cards at once, and the bottom one is not available for building until the top one has been played. The top card of the wastepile may be built if it becomes usable.

You may redeal the wastepile once. The game usually comes out.

Sly Fox

This relative of **Grandfather** comes from an old German book under the title **Die Schlaue**. It is a game of skill and can usually be expected to come out with proper play.

Follow the rules given above as far as the point at which you are ready to start turning cards from stock. Now, however, you deal another twenty cards to the promenade before pausing to continue play. These twenty must all be dealt – you may not build them as they come out. But they may be dealt to any or all positions of the promenade, as you please, there being no restriction on the number of cards held in each pile. There is no separate wastepile as such.

Continue by playing cards from the tops of the promenade piles to those of the Ace and King piles. Note that cards for building must come from the promenade, not from other Ace or King piles. When stuck, deal out twenty more again – or as many as are left – and play as before.

There is no redeal, but you are unlikely to want one in any case.

The Fly

This very old game is the two-pack version of **Demon** or **Canfield**.

Pick out the Aces and lay them in a row. Play to build them up to Kings regardless of suit. Deal the next thirteen cards face down as a reserve ('the fly'). Whenever the top card is face down, turn it face up. Turn cards from stock and either build them if possible or else discard them face up to any of five wastepiles. You may, at any time possible, build the top card of any wastepile or the reserve. There is no redeal. The game rarely comes out.

The Frog

A game almost identical to **The Fly**, except that it comes out even less often. Play as above, except:

(a) Do not set up all the Aces, but check through the thirteen-card reserve first (this reserve being known as 'the frog') and set up any that may be among them before starting play.

(b) Build the sequences up in suit (not regardless of suit).

Cabal (The Secret)

An old German game closely related to flies and frogs, but more likely to come out. It also resembles the excellent one-pack game **Strategy**.

Deal thirteen cards face down as a reserve called 'the secret' and turn the top one face up (and others one by one as they get uncovered).

Deal the next card face up to one side as the first base. Others of the same rank are to be founded as bases as and when they appear, and your aim is to build them all up into thirteen-card sequences (passing from King to Ace as necessary), regardless of suit.

Deal the next twelve cards face up in three rows of four as the start of twelve wastepiles collectively called 'the cabal'. Build as far as you can from the cabal and the secret, without replacing any cards taken.

When stuck, deal the rest of the cards face up onto any of the twelve wastepiles. (The original rules do not say whether you are allowed to build any as you go. I assume not, as the game is otherwise too easy.) Then try to complete the sequences by playing from these piles and the secret. There is no redeal.

Display

A nice game of rather unusual design. If you are left-handed, change everything around as necessary.

Deal a card face up to the top left of the table. Your aim is to make it the first of a row of thirteen cards forming an ascending suit sequence from left to right, passing from King to Ace as necessary. Also, this row is to be the first of eight similar rows, each in one suit, starting with the same rank on the left and forming an ascending sequence to the right.

Turn cards from stock one by one. Add each one to the display, provided that you can place it edge to edge with a card already in

Display   A game recently started. As the first card dealt was ♡J, each row will run Jack, Queen, King, Ace, Two . . . up to Ten on the right.

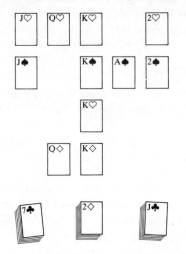

position. If not, discard it face up to any of three wastepiles. You may always play the top card of a wastepile later, if you can.

Having run out of stock, gather the wastepiles up without shuffling them, and run through them again as a new stock. This time, however, you discard to only one wastepile, and there is no redeal.

The game usually comes out all right.

Gemini

Another member of the preceding family of games, **Gemini** has one or two unusual features which make it interesting, if not exasperating.

Deal cards face up until you have four of different ranks and suits, and shuffle the rest back into the pack. These four are bases. Put them in a row with enough room for another card to go between each pair. Their four duplicates are also to be founded as bases, as and when they appear.

Your aim is to build each pair of bases up into two identical suit sequences, passing from King to Ace as necessary. Furthermore, each pair of bases must be built up at exactly the same rate. If they are Aces, for example, you can build a Two on one of them, but cannot add the Three until you have built the other Two.

Turn cards from stock one by one and either build them if possible or else discard them face up to any of five wastepiles. You may always build a card from the top of a wastepile if it becomes possible to do so.

If you get stuck after running out of cards, gather the wastepiles up and use them as a new stock, without reshuffling. Continue as before, but discarding to only two wastepiles instead of five.

There is no redeal, and the game does not often come out.

Tweedledum

In a variation on **Gemini**, which I call **Tweedledum**, of each pair of bases in the same suit one is to be built in ascending sequence and one in descending. Given Jacks, for example, one will be followed by Queen and built up to Ten, the other followed by Ten and built down to Queen. Here it is important to keep track of the number of cards in each pair of sequences, as again they must proceed at the same rate. At no time may one pile hold more than one card in excess of its twin.

Imaginary Thirteen (Calculation)

The final member of the 'grandfatherly' family is a two-pack version of **Calculation** and is closely related to **Mathematical** (or **Senior Wrangler**).

Take eight cards from Ace to Eight, regardless of suit, and put them in a row in numerical order. These are 'indicators', indicating the intervals by which the main sequences are to be built. Your aim is to found eight bases in a row beneath the indicators, as and when they appear, and to build each up into a thirteen-card sequence regardless of suit but by the interval prescribed by its indicator. Each base is to be twice the value of its indicator, so the bases will run: 2 4 6 8 10 Q A 3. Note that Queen counts as 12, Ace represents 14 and Three 16. Generally, any rank represents either its actual value or its actual value plus 13.

This aim is to be achieved by turning cards from stock and either building them if possible or else discarding them face up to any of four wastepiles. You may play from the top of the wastepiles whenever you can. There is no redeal.

For reference, the completed sequences will run as follows:

A	2	3	4	5	6	7	8	9	10	J	Q	K
2	4	6	8	10	Q	A	3	5	7	9	J	K
3	6	9	Q	2	5	8	J	A	4	7	10	K
4	8	Q	3	7	J	2	6	10	A	5	9	K
5	10	2	7	Q	4	9	A	6	J	3	8	K
6	Q	5	J	4	10	3	9	2	8	A	7	K
7	A	8	2	9	3	10	4	J	5	Q	6	K
8	3	J	6	A	9	4	Q	7	2	10	5	K

The first card in each of these rows is the indicator and the second its associated base.

Miss Milligan

This used to be a very popular patience on the English side of the Atlantic. Indeed, the late Professor Ross, an assiduous patience researcher when not exploring the fields of 'U and non-U' behaviour, which he invented, simply referred to it as 'the best patience' without further qualification. To which I can only say that Miss Milligan certainly has her attractions, but yielding to patient wooing more than once in a blue moon is not one of them.

Keep dealing eight cards face up in a row, overlapping previous cards or filling spaces as the case may be, and pausing after each deal to play as far as you can in accordance with the following rules.

Your aim is to release the Aces as and when they become available, and to build them up in suit and sequence to the Kings.

The exposed cards at the near ends of the columns may be taken for building, when possible, or packed on one another downwards in alternating colour (e.g. red Jack on black Queen, etc.). Cards may be moved singly or in any length of properly packed sequence. A space made by clearing out a column may be filled only with a King or a sequence headed by a King.

When all cards have been entered into the layout, and you have played as far as you can, and have got stuck – as nearly always happens – you continue the game by a process known as 'weaving' (or 'waiving', but 'weaving' is more descriptive). To do this, take out any exposed card and hold it to one side in reserve. Continue play, if you can, until you can either build the reserved card or pack it back into the tableau.

You may weave in and out of the tableau as often as you like, but if you get stuck with a card still in reserve the game is lost.

Giant

This German game, probably ancestral to **Miss Milligan**, is almost identical. Play as described above, but (*a*) a space on the tableau may be filled with any available card or packed sequence, not just a King, and (*b*) you may, if possible and desirable, 'worry back' a card from a main sequence into the tableau if you can find somewhere to pack it. These privileges greatly increase the chances of success.

Merry-go-Round

A Victorian game, very pictorial and descriptive, a little complicated, but requiring no great skill and turning out successfully more often than not.

Take out all the Kings, Queens and Jacks. Make a roundabout layout with eight spokes, each spoke consisting of a Queen on the inside followed by the King and then the Jack of the same suit (as illustrated).

The Queens represent the supports, the Kings the horses, and the Jacks are boys waiting to ride on the horses. (Why not girls? Well, I did warn you it was a Victorian game.) This they cannot do until they have paid the fare, which is represented by completing the building of a sequence of cards on each Jack.

Shuffle the rest of the cards and deal them out face up six at a time, placing two on each of three wastepiles. After each deal play what cards you can from the top of the wastepiles before dealing the next batch of six.

Wastepile cards may be played in two ways. First, if they cannot be entered into the layout as described below, they may be packed on one another upwards or downwards regardless of suit (e.g. on a Three you may pack any Two or Four). Second, and preferably, they may be used for building suit sequences on the Jacks. Upon each Jack found, as they become available, an Ace and a Ten of the

Merry-go-Round On each Jack you found an Ace and a Ten, then build the Ace up to the Five and the Ten down to the Six. The completed sequences are paid into the central 'till' and the Jack can then be placed on the King. As shown, cards are dealt in pairs to each of three wastepiles.

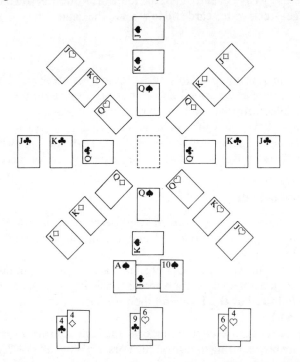

same suit as the Jack. Build the Ace up to the Five and the Ten down to the Six. When both sequences are complete, being headed by the matching Five and Six, you 'pay the fare' by placing both sequences in a pile ('the till') at the centre of the layout, and mounting the Jack (boy) on the adjacent King (horse).

If, within the layout, you have built up to the Five on one side, and the Six turns up before the Seven it needs to go on, you may temporarily place the Six on the Five and move it off again when possible. Similarly, a Five may be temporarily placed on a Six if it turns up before its Four.

If the game sticks after you have run out of cards, you may gather the wastepiles up into a new stock and play through it once again.

(This makes the game so easy that I suggest you deal to only one wastepile the second time around.)

Jubilee

More than one of her loyal subjects had the idea of composing a patience to commemorate Victoria's Golden Jubilee of 1887, with the result that there is more than one patience of the said title. This one comes from Lady Cadogan's second volume, published in the same year. It is eminently typical of its period.

Take out all the numeral hearts and arrange them (as illustrated) in the form of a heart surrounding a cross of Nines and Tens. In the middle of the cross put both Queens of hearts, one face down as a throne and one face up to represent the Queen. Beneath this display deal six random cards face up in a row. These form a tableau called 'the antechamber' (or 'anti-chamber', as Lady Cadogan has it).

Your aim is to release the other six Aces – two each of spades, clubs and diamonds – and build them up in suit and sequence to the

Jubilee   The opening layout.

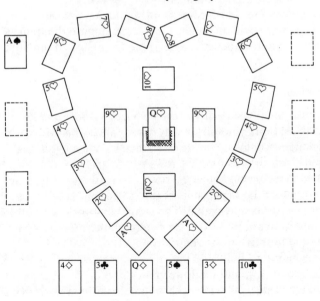

Tens, followed by Queens as the crowning card. Jacks and Kings are omitted from these sequences, being merely discarded into some decorative sideshow as and when they turn up in the play.

If any Aces appear in the antechamber, found them as bases on either side of the central display. Do any further building that may be possible from the antechamber, and fill gaps from stock.

Having played as far as you can, turn cards from stock one by one and either build them on the sequences or pack them on the antechamber if possible, or else discard them face up to a single wastepile. (Remember Jacks and Kings are eliminated altogether as they appear.)

Exposed cards of the antechamber may be built when possible or packed on one another in descending sequence regardless of suit. Only one card may be moved at a time. Since Jacks are not used, a Ten may be packed on a Queen. Since Kings are not used, a Queen may not be packed on anything. A gap made within the antechamber may be filled with any single available card. There is no redeal.

Lady Cadogan adds:

'The final tableau, if the game is successful, represents the SOVEREIGN enthroned in the HEART of her people.

The KINGS of the earth come from afar to do homage.

The QUEENS stand on either side to do honour to the JUBILEE.

All KNAVES are expelled and fly from the QUEEN's dominions.'

Muggins

This game bears a superficial resemblance to **Above and Below** (see page 100). I think you will see why it is so called when you get into it, though it does come out more often than its title may suggest.

Deal eight cards face up in a row. We will call this 'the row'. Deal the next card face up above the row. This card is the first base. The other seven of the same rank are also to be set out as bases as and when they become available. The second one goes below the row, the third above, and so on alternately, until you have four bases above and four below the central row.

Your aim is to build the upper bases into ascending sequences regardless of suit, and the lower bases into descending sequences regardless of suit – all sequences to contain thirteen cards, King and

Ace being consecutive where necessary. (Example: if the bases are Nines, the upper ones are to be built up to the Eights and the lower ones down to the Tens.)

Start by taking any of the cards in the row that can be founded as bases or added to a main sequence, and replace them from stock.

When stuck, both now and throughout the game, start dealing cards face up across the row from left to right. If any of the cards you deal are consecutive – either upwards or downwards – deal them to the same pile, and do not go on to the next pile until you turn a card which is no longer in sequence. Kings and Aces are consecutive, and a sequence may change direction on the same pile.

The top card of any pile may be taken for building, but not if it is the only card and would thereby make a gap in the row.

Having dealt all cards out, you may continue the game by packing top cards of the row on top of one another in sequence, regardless of suit and direction. You may not take the last card of a pile unless the game blocks, in which case you may then pack or build it if possible. This does not entitle you to take another last card – you must wait for the game to block again before you are free to do so.

There is no redeal.

Note: You are allowed to look through the piles to see what they contain.

Kings

This elderly but lively game comes from the unspecified German source plundered by Lady Cadogan in her second series of patience games.

Take out the Aces and arrange them in two columns of four each down the table. These are bases. Your aim is to build them all up into thirteen-card sequences headed by Kings, regardless of suit.

Start dealing cards from the stock one by one in a clockwise direction around the bases, i.e. down the right side and up the left of the Ace columns. To save space, overlap these cards in a horizontal direction.

If, at any time during the deal, the card you turn can be built on either of the Ace piles in the same horizontal line as itself, build it instead of dealing it, and pass on to the next position with the next card.

By the time you run out of cards you will (with any luck) have started building most of the main sequences. The unbuilt cards may now be taken for building or packing on one another, working always from the outside to the inside of a row. They may be built on any Ace piles, not necessarily the ones in the same row. Or any exposed card may be packed on any other, regardless of suit, so long as it is consecutive in either direction. A space made by emptying a row may be filled with any exposed card.

No redeal is allowed – or, to tell the truth, is likely to be needed.

Algerian Patience

I do not know why this game is so called, but it is a tough one to play until you get used to it.

Deal eight cards face up in a row near the top of the board. This starts the tableau. At the bottom, deal six fans of six cards each, also face up. These form a reserve. Only the top (exposed) card of each fan is available to start with.

Your aim is to found, at the very top of the board, an Ace and a King of each suit as they become available, and to build them respectively upwards and downwards into complete suit sequences.

Start by doing any building or packing that may be possible from the fourteen available cards. Cards in the tableau may be packed on one another in suit and sequence, going in either direction. Kings and Aces count as consecutive, so they can be packed on one another. Only one card may be moved at a time.

Exposed cards from the reserve may be built on the main sequences, packed on the tableau, or used for filling any spaces made in the tableau. But they themselves are not to be replaced or packed upon for the time being.

When stuck – or earlier, if you prefer – deal two more cards face up to the top of each fan in the reserve, then continue play as before. Do the same again whenever the game blocks, until you have only eight cards left in stock.

When only eight are left and the game blocks again, deal the last cards face up across the tableau, one to the end of each column.

There is no redeal, but a 'grace' is allowed as follows. Whenever a fan in the reserve is entirely cleared out, an exposed card from a column in the tableau may be taken out and held in its place until it can be built on a sequence or packed back into the tableau.

Vacuum

Vacuum has some interesting positional features which may compensate for its intransigence.

Separate the two packs and shuffle them individually. Take out the Aces and Kings from one of them. At the top of the board make a row of Aces on one side and a row of Kings on the other, leaving between the two lines a space equivalent to the width of three cards. This space, right down to the bottom of the board, is 'the vacuum'. Play to build the Aces up to the Kings and the Kings down to the Aces, in suit.

Deal the next eleven cards face up in a row to start the tableau. The first four of these will lie beneath the Aces, the next three within the vacuum, and the last four beneath the Kings.

If there is a Two lying immediately beneath an Ace of the same suit, or a Queen beneath a King of the same suit, you may build it. A Two or a Queen in the vacuum may be built on the appropriate base regardless of position. Fill any gaps from stock, and see if you can continue play. Again, you may build any card lying in the same vertical line as the sequence it continues, or any buildable card in the vacuum.

When stuck, continue dealing from the rest of the first pack followed by the whole of the second. Deal them face up across the eleven cards of the tableau, pausing after each card to see if it can be built. A card in line with a main sequence of its own suit may be built if it fits, as may any buildable card falling to the vacuum. The next card is then dealt in its place, unless it can also be built.

Cards which are already in the layout may be built in accordance with the same positional rules if they become exposed by the play of the cards covering them, but in this case they are not replaced.

The rules change when you run out of stock. You may now build exposed cards regardless of position, and pack them on one another upwards or downwards in suit, moving cards singly or in any length of properly packed sequence. A space made by clearing out a column may be filled with any available card or sequence. Cards may be reversed between Ace and King piles if they continue the sequence, though bases must not be moved from their original position.

Two redeals are allowed. To redeal, gather up all the columns from left to right, turn them upside down into a new stock, and deal again. During a deal, cards may only be built in accordance with the positional rules described above.

Mount Olympus

Another classic game, of German origin and transmitted through the medium of Lady Cadogan (Book 2), **Mount Olympus** is traditionally played in a rather inconvenient pictorial design, representing, of course, the home of the gods. The traditional layout is the upper one of the two shown opposite. Its disadvantage is the difficulty of spreading the columns towards you so that you can see what's going on. The lower one is my suggestion for a more practical alternative.

Take out all the Aces and Twos and set these sixteen cards out as bases. (In the original design they represent a semicircle of clouds surrounding the top of the mountain; in mine, they represent the mountain itself.)

Shuffle the rest of the pack and deal the next nine cards out, face up and not overlapping one another, to start the tableau. (In the original design they represent the mountain; in mine, they become the semicircle of clouds.)

The Aces and Twos are base cards. Your aim is to build them up in suit and alternating sequence so as to finish with Kings and Queens as gods and goddesses:

$$A \quad 3 \quad 5 \quad 7 \quad 9 \quad J \quad K$$
$$2 \quad 4 \quad 6 \quad 8 \quad 10 \quad Q$$

Build cards from the tableau to the main sequences whenever possible, and fill gaps from stock. On the tableau, exposed cards may be packed on one another in suit and descending alternating sequence (e.g. ♡9 on ♡J, etc.). For this purpose you may move cards singly or in any length of properly packed sequence. A gap may be filled with any available card from stock or tableau.

When stuck, deal another nine cards over the tableau, one to each position, and continue as before.

Mount Olympus In the traditional layout (above) it is awkward to spread the cards of the tableau towards you because they get in one another's way. In the alternative layout (below) they can be spread outwards as if radiating away from the central mountain.

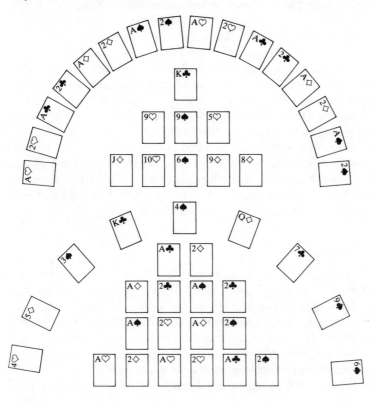

There is no redeal, but the game will usually come out with attentive play.

Rittenhouse

Derived from **Vacuum** by Capt. Jeffrey T. Spaulding, the noted African explorer, **Rittenhouse** requires a good deal of patience and looks as if it ought to come out more often than it does. But it doesn't.

Shuffle both packs together and deal a top row consisting of four

Aces, a space, and four Kings. Your aim is to build the Aces up to Kings and the Kings down to Aces, regardless of suit.

Deal cards in rows of nine under this top line, the first four of each going under the Aces and the last four under the Kings. During the deal, if a card can be built on a sequence in the same vertical line as the position it is going to, build it and deal the next card in its place. A card falling to the centre column may be built wherever it fits.

The deal finished, exposed cards at the ends of columns may be packed on one another in sequence regardless of suit. Sequences may go up or down and change direction as often as you like in the same line. Only one card may be moved at a time. A space made by emptying a column may be filled with any exposed card.

The catch is that the same positional restriction on building applies throughout the game. That is, an exposed card may only be built on the sequence with which it is vertically in line (i.e. the one at the head of its column). As before, however, the end card of the centre column may be built wherever it fits.

Nationale

Found an Ace and a King of each suit in a row. Play to build the Aces up to the Kings and the Kings down to the Aces, following suit.

Deal cards face up, not in rows but in columns, one beneath each base card. Each column is to take eight cards, but if a card about to be dealt can be built on the sequence at the head of its column, build it instead, and that will shorten the column by one card. Any previously dealt card thus exposed may also be built.

Having dealt, pack exposed cards on one another in suit and sequence. Only one card may be moved at a time, but sequences may change direction in the same column. Exposed cards may be built on any of the sequences.

Fill an empty column with any exposed card. There is no redeal.

St Helena

Also known as **Napoleon's Favourite**, this classic usually succeeds.

Take a King and an Ace of each suit. Lay the four Kings in a row and the Aces in a row beneath them. Play to build them respectively downwards and upwards into thirteen-card suit sequences.

St Helena The start of a game. The third card dealt can be built immediately on ♣K and will be replaced with the next card from stock.

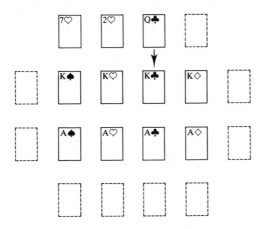

Deal cards around them in clockwise rotation to twelve positions. The first four go from left to right above and in line with the Kings, two go down the right side, four beneath the Aces from right to left, two more up the left-hand side, and so on.

During the deal, if a card due to enter the top row can be built on a King pile, build it, and deal the next card in its place. A card to the bottom row may be built on an Ace pile if it fits, and a card falling to either side may be built on any of the main sequences.

After the deal, all exposed cards may be built on any sequences they fit, and may be packed on one another in suit and ascending or descending sequence. Only one card may be moved at a time, and Kings are not consecutive with Aces. Fill a gap with any available card.

Two redeals are allowed. For each, gather up the piles in reverse order of dealing, make a new stock of them and start dealing again in accordance with the same positional rules.

Four Corners

The last in a series of 'positional' patiences begun with **Vacuum**.

Your aim is to found an Ace and a King of each suit, as they become available, and to build them respectively upwards and

Four Corners

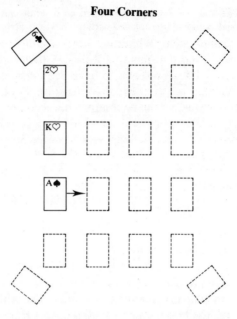

downwards into thirteen-card suit sequences. They are to be placed in two columns down the centre on the board, with Aces on the left and Kings on the right.

Start dealing cards in rotation down the left-hand side and up the right-hand side of where the base cards will go. Six are to be dealt on each side, the top and bottom ones at an angle ('corners'), the four central ones in line with the four (eventual) Aces and Kings.

During the deal, any base cards that turn up may be put in position immediately. Cards about to be dealt to a corner may be built wherever they fit. Cards about to be dealt to a side may be built if they are in horizontal line with the sequence they fit. Any card so dealt is replaced with the next one from stock.

After the deal, exposed cards may be built regardless of position, and may be packed on one another in sequence regardless of suit and direction (e.g. on a Five pack any Four or Six). Kings and Aces are consecutive, and a space may be filled with any available card.

Two redeals are allowed. For each, gather up the piles in reverse order of dealing, make a new stock of them, and start again in accordance with the rules of dealing described above.

Kaiser Bill

This game comes from Whitmore Jones's collection, where it appears under its more formal title **Kaiser Wilhelm**. Neither it nor the closely related **Tramp** seems to have been perpetuated in any recent collections, and I wonder if this is because they take up rather a lot of space – more than can be comfortably accommodated on the average card-table, if people still use such things. But the two games are quite distinctive, very challenging, and well worth knowing.

Deal 27 cards face up in three rows of nine. Do not overlap the rows, and keep all the cards well spaced out. Regard the resulting tableau as nine columns of three.

The object is to found all the Aces, as and when they become available, and to build them up in suit and sequence to the Kings.

Throughout play, the only cards available for founding and building are those at the bottom of their columns. Thus all those in the bottom row are available to start with. Removing one of them releases the one above it, and so on.

Start by founding any Aces that may be in the bottom row and doing any building that may be possible from the cards available, but without filling any gaps.

You may also pack cards on one another downwards in suit. For this purpose a card anywhere in the tableau may be packed on a suitable card anywhere else, regardless of its position in row or column. Cards may be taken for packing singly or in any length of packed sequence, so long as they always come from the top of a pile. The piles made by packing may be spread towards you so that all are visible (which is why they should be spaced out to start with.)

When you can't (or won't) play any further, deal 27 more cards over the layout in the same order as the first lot, i.e. along the top row first, and so on, covering packets, single cards or spaces as the case may be. Continue play as before, remembering that cards may be packed from any position to any other in the tableau, but only those from lowest position in their columns may be taken for building on the Ace piles.

Only 24 cards will be left on the last deal, so it will peter out along the bottom row. There is no other redeal and no 'grace' if you get stuck. But the game should come out more often than not with careful play.

Tramp

I have resisted the temptation to rename this game **Charlie Chaplin**, though it makes a nice companion piece to **Kaiser Bill** (opposite). It is a rather less friendly game, with a bit of a sting in its tail, and does not come out as often as you might like. Perhaps the previous game should be **Charlie Chaplin** and this one **Kaiser Bill**. But it is a good game, whatever you call it.

Deal 36 cards face up in four rows of nine, and the 37th face *down* to one side as a reserve. Do not overlap the rows, and keep all cards well spaced out. Regard the resulting tableau as nine columns of four.

The object is to found all the Aces, as and when they become available, and to build them up in suit and sequence to the Kings.

Throughout play, the only cards available for founding and building are those at the bottom of their columns. Thus all those in the bottom row are available to start with. Removing one of them releases the one above it, and so on.

Start by founding any Aces that may be in the bottom row and doing any building that may be possible from the cards available, but without filling any gaps.

You may also pack cards on one another downwards in suit. For this purpose a card anywhere in the tableau may be packed on any suitable card in the same or a lower row, but not in a higher one. Cards may be taken for packing singly or in any length of packed sequence, so long as they always come from the top of a pile.

When you can't (or won't) play any further, deal 36 more cards over the layout in the same order as before, and a 37th face down to one side with the previous reserve card. Deal to the top row first, and so on, covering packets, single cards or spaces as the case may be. Continue play as before, remembering that cards may be packed anywhere except on higher rows, and that only those from the lowest position in their columns may be taken for building on the Ace piles.

When ready, deal 27 of the last remaining cards over the first three rows of the tableau, and add the other three to the reserve. The five cards of the reserve ae now turned face up and are all available for entering into the game by packing or building whenever possible. They are not replaced and there is no redeal.

Phalanx (Quinzaine)

Also known as **Fifteen in a Row**, this game appears under its French title in an English book (Whitmore Jones) and under its Greek name in an American one (Dick's). All suitably describe its stolid, large-scale nature. It is a no-frills, no-nonsense game of pure skill, though I have to admit that even with perfect play it will not always come out. It is, in effect, a two-pack version of such games as **Baker's Dozen**, described earlier.

Deal fifteen cards face up in a row. Keep dealing rows of fifteen across and overlapping previous ones until you run out of cards. There will only be fourteen in the seventh row.

The object is to release an Ace and a King of each suit, as and when they become available, and to build them respectively upwards and downwards into thirteen-card suit sequences.

Start by founding any uncovered Aces and Kings. If there are none in the bottom row, you may extract them from the second row up.

The exposed card at the near end of each column may be taken for building a main sequence or for packing on another exposed card. Pack cards in suit and sequence, moving only one card at a time. Sequences may ascend or descend, and may change direction in the same column. Aces and Kings are not consecutive.

A space made by clearing out a column may be filled with any exposed card. Or – often more helpfully – it may be filled in the following way. Take all the exposed cards of a given suit, arrange them in ascending or descending numerical order, and make a column of them in the vacancy.

Grace: If the game seizes up completely, you may lift any exposed card and take the one beneath it for packing or building. This grace may be taken once only during the course of a game, and only when no other move can be made.

Heads and Tails (Regiment)

A jolly good game, this, which should come out as often as not.

Deal three rows of eight cards each, not overlapping: the first row face up, the second face down, the third face up. Deal the rest of the cards face down across the middle row until it consists of eight piles,

Heads and Tails A game in progress. The gap in the bottom row is filled with the top card of the second pile from the left.

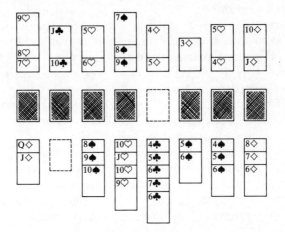

with eleven in each. The face-up cards are the start of a tableau. The object is to release an Ace and a King of each suit, as and when they become available, and to build them respectively upwards and downwards into thirteen-card suit sequences.

Exposed cards of the tableau may be taken for building main sequences, or for packing on one another in suit and sequence. Only one card may be moved at a time, and Aces are not consecutive with Kings, but sequences may ascend, descend or both as much as you like in the same column.

Fill any vacancy with the top card of the central pile aligned vertically with it. Or, if all cards of that pile have been taken, from the nearest pile to the left of the gap. Or, if none, from the furthest pile to its right. There are no redeals or graces.

House on the Hill

This close relative of **Fan** is presumably so called because the overall fan-shape is dealt upside down, as I have shown it here. (If you can think of a better reason, write and let me know.)

Deal 34 three-card fans and two one-card fans. Aim to release the Aces and build them up in suit and sequence to the Kings.

House on the Hill   An opening deal.

Exposed cards of the fans may be taken for building or for packing on one another. Pack downwards in suit, moving only one card at a time. Empty fans are not replaced. There are no redeals or graces, but the game usually succeeds without them.

Rainbow

Another member of the 'fan' club represented by such games as **Fan** and **House on the Hill**. They all involve dealing cards out in fans or sweeps of three or four cards at a time. Technically, these act just like the ordinary but longer columns in most games but they make for more attractive designs and usually offer more scope for

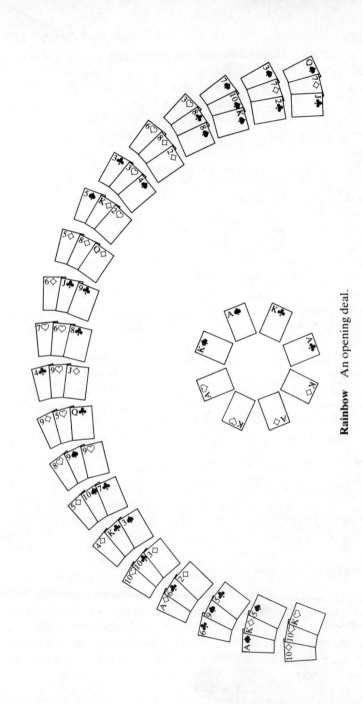

Rainbow An opening deal.

different lines of play. **Rainbow** is particularly pretty, though it does not come out all that often.

Pick out an Ace and a King of each suit to act as bases. (I like to arrange them in a circle representing the sun, as illustrated, even if it defies meteorological verisimilitude.) The object is to build them respectively upwards and downwards into thirteen-card suit sequences.

Next, deal 20 three-card fans in an arc around the bases. These form the tableau. The exposed card of each fan at any given time is available for building on the main sequences or for packing on another exposed card. Pack upwards or downwards in suit, changing direction as often as you like in the same fan. Only one card may be moved at a time, and Aces are not consecutive with Kings. Cards may be transferred from Ace to King piles and vice versa, though the bases must always be left in place.

Whenever a fan is emptied of cards, replace it at once with a new three-card fan dealt from stock. This is the only way in which fresh cards can be entered into the game, so it is important to empty fans whenever you get the chance.

If the game seizes up, you may exercise the following 'grace'. Take the exposed card of each fan and slip it to the buried end of its fan, and then continue play. This grace may be taken not more than three times in the course of a single game.

Robin Post

This remarkably attractive game by Col G. H. Latham comes from the original *Card Games for One* by George Hervey. Unfortunately, his rules do not cover all eventualities and I have had to fill some gaps with my own suggestions.

Deal 52 cards face up in non-overlapping rows of 4, 5, 6, 7, 8, 7, 6, 5, and 4 cards. Arrange them corner to corner in the overall shape of a hexagon, as illustrated.

The object is to found an Ace and a King of each suit, as and when they become available, and to build them respectively upwards and downwards into thirteen-card suit sequences.

A card whose four corners are all touching other cards is blocked and cannot be used in any way. A card with three corners touching cannot be moved but may be packed upon. Any other card may be

Robin Post   An opening layout.

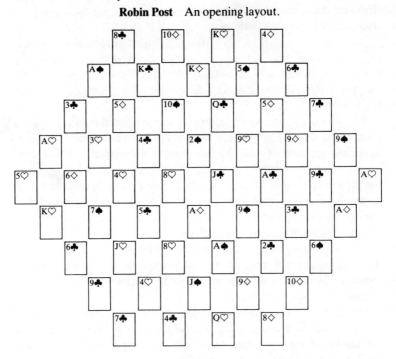

taken for building the main sequences or for packing on unblocked cards.

Pack in alternating colour (red on black, black on red) and either ascending or descending sequence. Aces and Kings are not consecutive, and you may not pack in both directions on the same pile.

The original rules continue: 'A sequence in the layout if movable may be moved as a whole but not in part, and may be reversed only onto a single card'.* Cards may be reversed from an Ace-pile to the King-pile of the same suit, and vice versa, but Ace and King bases must be left in position.

The other 52 cards may be dealt at any time. They must be dealt in

---

* The implications of this are nonsensical. If you can play a card singly to a pile of cards, which you evidently can, then you can reverse a sequence to a pile by counting it as a series of separate moves. I believe the 'single card' restriction is intended to apply to the dumping of a sequence as a unit, not to its card-by-card reversal.

the same order as before, covering single cards, packets or gaps as the case may be. All must be dealt before you continue play. There are no redeals or 'graces', but the game can usually be expected to come out with proper play.

Zodiac

The following game comes from the earliest English patience book and looks at first sight like a typical Victorian monstrosity – perhaps explaining why it has not been recorded very often since. Closer examination proves it to be a quite demanding game of skill, which should present you with a long-lasting challenge. It belongs to the same family as **Strategy** and **Grandfather**, in which no building of main sequences is done until all cards have been entered into the layout. The skill lies in entering them in such a way that they can eventually all be played off in the required order.

Deal eight cards face up in a row to form a reserve called 'the equator'. Deal 24 cards face up in a circle around them to form a tableau called 'the zodiac'.

Your eventual aim is to found an Ace and a King of each suit and to build them respectively up and down into thirteen-card suit sequences. Do not found or build any cards until further notice.

Turn cards from stock one by one and pack them if possible or else discard them face up to a single wastepile. The top card of the wastepile remains available for packing until covered by the next.

The 24 cards of the zodiac may be packed upon in suit and sequence. Sequences may go up and down ad lib in the same line, but Ace and King are not consecutive.

Cards may be packed from the stock, the wastepile or the equator, but once packed in the zodiac they must remain in position for the rest of the game. They may *not* be packed from one zodiac position to another.

A card taken from the equator may be replaced from stock or wastepile, so there always remain eight in reserve.

Having run out of stock, turn the wastepile and deal through it again. Do this as often as necessary until all cards have been entered into the layout. (If you cannot get them all in, you have lost already.)

When all have been entered into the layout, build four Ace-up

Zodiac   A game in progress.

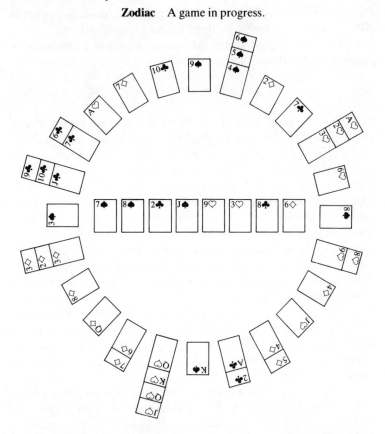

and four King-down suit sequences by taking cards one at a time from the ends of the zodiac piles or from the equator, as the case may be.

A card once built may not be transferred to a sequence of the same suit going in the opposite direction. If you have packed all the cards properly the game will come out; but the task is extremely difficult and no 'grace' is offered in the event of failure.

Cromwell

Another gem from the mind of Charles Jewell.

Deal all the cards out in 26 fans of four each. Your aim is to release all the Aces and build them up in suit and sequence to the Kings.

Exposed cards of the fans may be taken for building, or packed on one another downwards in suit. A whole or part sequence of properly packed cards may be moved as a unit. A space made by emptying a fan is not to be filled, and there is no redeal.

One 'grace' may be taken by exchanging the positions of *any* two cards in the layout. If no Aces are exposed on the opening deal, you'll have to use this grace up to get the game going.

Buffalo Bill

This is my improvement (I hope) on a game described by Mary Whitmore Jones under the title 'Little Billee'.

Deal all the cards out in 26 fans of four cards each.

Your aim is to found an Ace and a King of each suit, as and when they become available, and to build them respectively upwards and downwards into thirteen-card suit sequences.

The exposed card of each fan may be taken for building on a sequence. Or it may be taken out and held in reserve until it can be built. Up to eight cards may be held out at any one time.

Reserve cards cannot be entered back into the fans. Emptied fans are not replaced. There is no grace and no redeal. But the game can usually be expected to come out with proper play.

As a challenge, you may like to reduce the maximum number of cards that may be held in reserve at the same time.

PART THREE

Games for Three or More Packs

Games for Three or More Packs

Algerine

For 2–6 packs

This game bears some resemblances to **Tramp**, which may or may not explain its being named after a pirate – probably not, now I come to think of it. The original recommendation is for four to six packs, but you can try it with two or three just to get the flavour.

Shuffle one pack separately and the others all together. Deal the single pack face up in four rows of thirteen, keeping the rows separate from one another. This forms the tableau.

The object is to found all the Aces of all the packs, as and when they become available, and to build them up in suit and sequence to the Kings.

Throughout play, only cards in the bottom row are available for starting or continuing the main sequences. The play of such a card releases the one immediately above it in the next row, and so on up the column.

Cards in the tableau may be packed on one another in descending sequence and alternating colour (e.g. red Seven on black Eight, etc.), either singly or in any length of packed sequence.* But a card may only be packed onto another lying in the same or a higher row, never in a lower one.

Do not fill spaces in the tableau until an entire column has been emptied. You may then transfer to the top position of that column a single card from anywhere in the tableau – 'single' meaning one that has no other card on top of or beneath it.

Play as far as you can from the opening position. Then turn cards from stock one by one and either build or pack them if possible or else discard them face up to any of three wastepiles. The top card of every wastepile remains available for building or packing, and should be taken whenever possible as there is no redeal. You may

* I have arbitrarily assumed this to be the case, though my source – Whitmore Jones – says nothing about it one way or the other.

not, however, fill a vacancy from the top of a wastepile (or from stock).

Since there is no redeal, and no grace is provided if the game blocks, **Algerine** cannot be expected to come out very often.

Cable

For 3 packs

I believe **Cable** is so called because the three packs are supposed to represent three strands entwining together. It must have been invented by a member of a seafaring nation.

Separate the three packs and shuffle each one individually. Start the tableau by dealing the first pack out in five rows of ten, overlapping the rows to save space. Lay the last two cards face down to one side as a reserve. Take the second pack and continue the tableau by adding five more rows of ten to the first lot. Again, lay the last two cards face down to one side. (The four down-cards form a reserve and have no part to play until the game seizes up.)

Your aim is to found all twelve Aces, as and when they become available, and to build them up in suit and sequence to the Kings.

Exposed cards in the tableau may be taken for building or packing. They are to be packed on one another downwards in suit, either singly or in any length of properly packed sequence. A gap made by emptying a column may be filled with any available card or sequence.

When ready, turn cards from the third pack and either build or pack them if possible or else discard them face up to a single wastepile. The top card of the wastepile remains available for packing or building.

Having run out of stock, you may turn the wastepile and deal through it once again.

When the game blocks completely, as it is bound to do sooner or later, turn the four reserve cards face up in hope of freeing it. All remain available for building or packing as and when the opportunity arises, but if none of them can be entered as soon as they are

Games for Three or More Packs

turned then the game is lost. It does not, in fact, come out very often.

Barton

For 4 packs

A fairly conventional but challenging game to play if you have four packs and cannot think what else to do with them. You will rarely succeed in building all sixteen sequences – eight, according to Miss Whitmore Jones, is a reasonable objective – but you can give yourself a score out of sixteen for the number you do complete, and then try to break records on further attempts.

Shuffle all the packs together and deal six rows of seventeen cards each, face up. Don't overlap the rows, but space them as far apart as the table allows.

Your object is to release all sixteen Aces, as and when they become available, and to build them up in suit and sequence to the Kings.

Cards may only be taken for building from the lowest position in any of the seventeen columns. At start of play, therefore, only cards in the bottom row are available; but when one is taken, it frees the one above it, and so on up the column. When a column is emptied, any exposed card may be taken to fill its topmost position, but none may be put below it.

Cards in the tableau may be packed on one another downwards in suit. Only one card may be moved at a time, and it may come from any position in the layout, but it may only be packed onto a card or sequence in a *higher* row than itself. This means that cards in the top row cannot be moved at all until they are freed for building, while those in the bottom row are immediately available for building or packing but cannot themselves be packed on.

Having packed and built as far as you can and wish, continue play by turning cards from stock one by one. Pack or build them if possible, otherwise discard them face up to a single wastepile. The top card of the wastepile remains available for packing and building, and should be taken whenever possible as there is no redeal.

Empress of India

For 4 packs

Take out all the black Aces and Queens and all the red Kings and Jacks. Arrange them as illustrated, with a packet of Queens at top middle of the board surrounded by Jacks, Kings and Aces in a suitably symmetrical pattern.

Your aim is to build the Aces up in suit to the Kings (omitting Queens) and the Kings down in suit to the Aces (omitting Jacks). The sequences are short because half the Jacks and Queens are out of play.

Next, deal a tableau of cards face up in four rows of twelve, without overlapping. Put all red cards that turn up in the top two rows and all black cards in the bottom two. When you have completed both rows of one colour, discard any more of them that turn up to a wastepile until you have filled out the two rows of the other colour.

You may only build cards on the Ace and King piles by taking two at a time from the tableau. Each pair must consist of one red and one black card totalling 13 between them, counting 12 for a King and 11 for a Queen or Jack. (For example, you cannot build a black Two until you can simultaneously build a red Queen, and so on.) Building a pair of cards creates two spaces in the tableau, which you may then fill from stock or waste as the case may be. Cards from stock and waste may never be built onto the main sequences directly but must pass through the tableau first.

Spaces may also be created by packing card pairs in the tableau which cannot be built yet but will go together later. For example, you may pack a black Six on a red Seven, or vice versa, and leave them in position until they can be built.

Having played as far as you can from the opening deal, continue play by turning cards from stock one by one. Use them to fill gaps in the tableau, remembering that gaps in the upper two rows are for red cards and those in the lower two for black. If there are no suitable gaps, discard them face up to either of two wastepiles, one for each colour.

Gaps may also be filled from the tops of the wastepiles. Lose no opportunity to play from the wastepiles, as there is no redeal.

Empress of India Opening layout. Aces and Kings are bases for twelve-card suit sequences. In the tableau, the two rows of red cards represent 'the Army', those of black cards 'the Navy'.

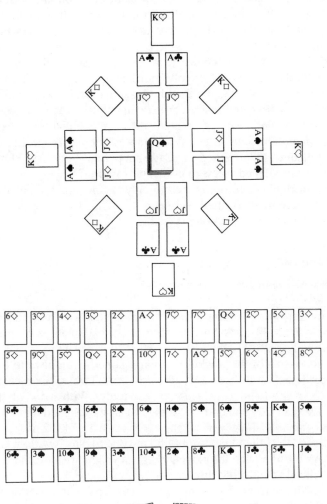

Note: When pairing cards in the tableau you have a choice of packing red on black or black on red. Having chosen, you may not later switch them round in order to transfer a gap from one colour to another. This is one of the few choices of play you are presented with during the game, which otherwise requires so little skill and so frequently comes out as to present little occasion for self-respect.

Empress of India has been represented as something of an historical mystery. It comes from the earliest English patience book, Lady Cadogan's first collection, of which the second edition (the only one known to the British Museum Library) was published in 1875. The first edition must have been published at least a couple of years earlier. Yet, as pointed out by the Italian card expert Giampaolo Dossena, Queen Victoria was not instated as Empress of India until 1876. 'Was Lady Cadogan psychic?', he asks. 'Or did she have privileged access to inside information?'

An intriguing question. One can only assume that the possibility of her becoming so titled had been in the air for some time and came as a surprise to no-one.

Boomerang

For two 32-card packs

Many European and some American card games are played with a short pack of 32 cards. Such cards are to be had over the counter in most countries other than Britain. Here, if you want to play **Piquet** or **Skat** – two of the world's best card games – you have to buy a 52-card pack and throw out all cards from Two to Six inclusive, which may offend your sense of economy. With a bit of luck, though, you may still find a boxed set of cards designed for another great game, **Bézique**, which happens to use a double 32 pack, or 64 cards in all. If then you cannot find anyone to play it with, you can always use the pack for playing the following patience devised by Morehead and Mott-Smith.

Deal three rows of four cards each, face up and not overlapping. This starts the tableau. Your aim is to found one Seven of each suit, as and when it appears, and to build it into a sixteen-card suit sequence in the following order:

7 8 9 10 J Q K A K Q J 10 9 8 7 A

If there are any Sevens in the tableau, take them out and build on them as far as you can, using whatever cards are visible. Replace all cards immediately from stock.

Cards in the tableau may also be packed on one another in suit and either ascending or descending sequence, though not both upwards and downwards in the same packet. When packing upwards, an Ace can go on a King but nothing can then go on the Ace. If there is an unpacked Ace in the tableau, you can pack in either direction on it – that is, K Q J, etc. or 7 8 9, etc. Only one card may be moved at a time.

There are no wastepiles, redeals, graces or second chances. With proper play, however, you can expect to bring the game out as often as not.

Olga

For four 32-card packs

The exotic **Olga** uses four short packs, making 128 cards in all. It comes from the second volume of Lady Cadogan, whose somewhat sketchy rules have required me to fill up one or two gaps.

The object is to found all sixteen Aces as and when they become available – eight down each side of the board – and to build them up in suit and sequence to the Kings thus:

$$A \ 7 \ 8 \ 9 \ 10 \ J \ Q \ K$$

Deal seven rows of seven cards each, without overlapping. Deal rows alternately face up (1st, 3rd, 5th, 7th) and face down (2nd, 4th, 6th). When dealing a face up row, you may immediately found any Ace which turns up and deal the next card in its place. Any other card you turn which can be built on an already-started Ace pile may also be built, and is replaced with the next card from stock. But once you have dealt a card without building it, you must leave it in place for the rest of the deal.

Having dealt, examine the tableau before going through the rest of the pack, and make any useful moves that may present themselves. Cards may be built only from the lowest position in a column – that is, only from the bottom row to start with. The play of a bottom card releases the one above it for building, and so on up the

Olga   An opening deal.

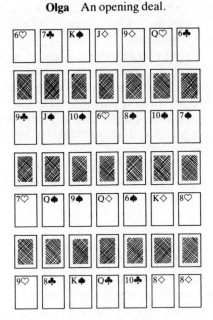

column. Whenever you thereby release a down-card, turn it face up.

Any faced card in the tableau may be packed on any other, downwards and in alternating colour (e.g. red Seven on black Eight, etc.). Only one card may be moved at a time, but the top of a packet may be packed elsewhere if it fits – a point well worth remembering.

When ready, turn cards from stock and either build or pack them if possible or else discard them face up to a single wastepile. The top of the wastepile remains available for building or packing, and should be taken whenever possible as there is no redeal.

A space in the tableau may be filled only with a King, taken from waste, stock or elsewhere in the tableau.

Remember that you may only build from the *lowest* position in any column – not merely from a card or packet lying above a space.

The game can usually be expected to come out with careful play.

Select Bibliography

Only those books are listed which contain useful or original contributions to the subject. Some of those listed are out of print and only available from libraries.

Cadogan, Adelaide: *Illustrated Games of Patience* (Sampson Low *et al.*, 2nd edition, 1875, republished in facsimile 1968 by Leslie Frewin).

Cadogan, Adelaide: *Illustrated Games of Patience – Second Series* (Sampson Low *et al.*, 1887).

'Cavendish' (Jones, Henry): *Patience* (De la Rue, 1890).

Hervey, George: *Teach Yourself Card Games for One* (Hodder & Stoughton, 1965).

Morehead, Albert, and Mott-Smith, Geoffrey: *The Complete Book of Patience* (Faber & Faber, 1950).

Parlett, David: *The Penguin Book of Patience* (Allen Lane/Penguin, 1979).

Whitmore Jones, Mary: *Games of Patience, Series 1–5* (Upcott Gill, 1899).

Whitmore Jones, Mary: *New Games of Patience* (Upcott Gill, 1911).

Whitmore Jones, Mary, revised by Laurence Morton: *Popular Games of Patience* 3rd edition (The Bazaar, Exchange and Mart, undated).

Glossary of Technical Terms

Alternating colour Describes a sequence of cards which are alternately red (hearts or diamonds) and black (spades or clubs).

Available Describes a card which you are allowed to build, pack or move to another position. (See also **buried**.) Typically available are: the top card of stock, the top card of the wastepile, the uncovered card at the bottom of each column, and any card held in a reserve.

Base The start card of a main sequence which you are required to build – typically an Ace or a King.

Board The playing surface.

Build To add a card or cards to a main sequence.

Buried Describes a card which is wholly or partly covered by one or more cards and therefore not 'available' for moving.

Column A line of cards running north-south of the board with short edges parallel (sometimes overlapping one another to save space).

Court cards King, Queen, Jack.

Down-card One which is lying face down.

Exposed Describes a card which is not wholly or partly covered by another and is therefore 'available'.

Fan Three or four cards spread out and overlapping one another in the shape of a fan.

Found To take a base card and put it in position ready to build a main sequence on it.

Grace A special move that may be made to free a blocked game.

Layout A pattern or arrangement of cards made on the opening deal, before any are played. It may consist of a tableau or reserve or both.

Numeral Any card from Ace to Nine, as opposed to a 'court'.

Pack To lay cards on one another in accordance with the rules governing how they may go together (e.g. in sequence, in suit, in alternating colour, etc.). The difference between packing and building (see entry above) is that packing takes place in the layout and is a temporary measure designed to get the cards partly ordered so that they can then be built more easily.

Packet A pile of cards, especially if they have been packed on one another rather than merely dealt as they come.

Rank The face value of a card. Each suit has thirteen ranks.

Redeal To take up the wastepile, turn it face down, and use it as a new stockpile in order to continue the game.

Release To make a card 'available', e.g. by removing a card which is covering or otherwise blocking it.

Reserve A group of cards dealt or moved to a special part of the layout. How they are used depends on the rules of the individual game. Generally, the difference between a reserve and a tableau is that no packing takes place on a reserve.

Reverse To transfer a card from the top of an ascending sequence to the top of a descending sequence if it fits either. Some games allow reversals to be carried out from one main sequence to another.

Row A line of cards running east-west across the board with long edges parallel (sometimes overlapped to save space).

Sequence Ascending sequence runs A 2 3 and so on up to King; descending sequence runs K Q J, etc. down to Ace. In many games the sequence is cyclic, so that King-Ace are regarded as consecutive. 'Main' sequences are the ones which it is the object of the game to build.

Stock Cards left in hand when those required for the opening layout have been dealt. The stock should be held face down in one hand, though the top card – which is always 'available' – may be turned face up while the player considers whether to use it immediately or make some useful preparatory moves first. Some say that the stock may always be held face up, thus saving unnecessary wrist movement. Usually, it makes little difference which method is followed. But there are some games in which it does make a difference and the stock *must* be held face down. Also, if they are held face up, there is a greater temptation to 'cheat' by spreading them slightly in order to see whether or not a particular card is likely to come up in the next few moves. Only by holding the stock face down can you be sure of never going wrong.

Tableau An arrangement of cards in the layout, usually in rows or columns, sometimes forming a decorative or representational pattern. See also **reserve**.

Up-card A card which is lying face up.

Wastepile Usually, a pile of cards to which those that cannot be entered into the game are discarded – a rubbish heap. The top card of such a wastepile is always 'available' until it is covered by the next discard. It has a slightly different meaning as applied to a family of games (e.g. **Strategy**) in which two or more so-called wastepiles take the place of a layout.

Index